NOW! WE'RE HAVING FUN

Humorous Anecdotes of Life On The Last Frontier

by Ted H. Leonard

illustrated by Jamie Smith

ALASKA WORD WORKS PUBLISHING COMPANY
Salcha, Alaska

PUBLISHED BY ALASKA WORD WORKS PUBLISHING COMPANY
P.O. Box 51
Salcha, Alaska 99714

First printing June 1994 USA
Revised edition August,1997 USA
Library of Congress Catalog Card Number 94-094456
ISBN 0-9641553-1-1

The individual columns in this book first appeared in the following Alaskan newspapers: the NORTH POLE INDEPENDENT, THE CURRENT DRIFT and ALASKA OUTDOORS.

Illustrations by Jamie appear in this book on pages 7, 30, 37, 43, 50, 66, 80, 89, 103, 107, 121, 129, 139, 155 and, of course, on the cover.

Dedicated with love to Plum (short for sugar plum, the wife)...previously known to the rest of the world as Dottie Leonard.

FOREWORD

We have a lot of fun, here in Alaska's wild interior. The opportunities for outdoor fun are why many of us have chosen to live here...'though, at times, we do things in the name of fun that would cause any sane person from "Outside" (anywhere not in Alaska) to conclude that we all must be complete idiots.

Indeed, we may need to be reminded that we're having fun. Like when we ride our snow machines down the wrong side of the hill, into an impassible valley. As we spend the next six or eight hours dragging the suddenly heavy (at least a ton, it seems) machines back up the hill, through four feet of soft snow, and onto the trail, we pause to look at each other with sheepish grins and say witty things like, "Remind me how much fun we're having." or, "When does the fun start?"...well, half witty, maybe.

To me, the best time of year is that short few months when we have liquid water...and boating. Then is when we can really have fun (Teddy Roosevelt called it strenuous living).

Here's one of my favorite stories about that kind of fun:

One hunting season, Sid Sanford and his hunting partner, Little Joe Fletcher (a couple of local characters), came by airboat to the Tanana Flats. Now, to get into the Flats they had to wriggle their way up a small creek (in the boat, of course), wind up the boat's engine to full power, and jump the boat up over a six foot high, steep, mud bank, through a thicket of cattail stalks and over a beaver dam, to splash down in the swamp.

I had stopped my boat to rest, a bit, when we heard Sid's boat coming. The engine sound came closer and closer until, finally, Sid and Little Joe rocketed over the top of the bank – at least 2 feet of air visible under the boat's bottom. The flight was short lived, as they splashed down in a spray of black, stinking mud, followed by a shower of cattail fuzz and stalks. Little Joe, jolted from his seat, disappeared into the bottom of the boat. Let me tell you, that splash down would have made the astronauts at Canaveral nervous.

Well, Sid pulled up on the grass beside us and stopped, dripping black goo caked with fuzz from his face and shoulders. Joe struggled out of the bottom of the boat and back upright, also dripping, a cattail clenched in his teeth.

They looked like they had been tarred and feathered...but Little Joe spat out the cattail, dashed the mud from his eyes, grinned and said "NOW! we're havin' fun."

And it's true...despite all the difficulties we get into, sinking boats, bad weather, broke down boats, stranded for a week, unfriendly meetings with bears, stuck snow machines or snow machines through the

ice and into the river, we are having fun. We must
be...or we wouldn't keep doing it...would we?
 I wrote my following poem on the upper Salcha
River, after a week long rain:

NOW! WE'RE HAVING FUN
(an Alaskan saying, in times of adversity)
Dreary, dark, dismal, dripping,
from sullen brooding skies;
daunting, drenching, steady rain,
upon the foliage sighs.
From each leaf, each tree and bush,
damp, dank drizzles drain.
Grim, grey, gulches gushing rain,
rain puddles on the flat,
mushy, moldy, squishy moss,
and on the creek, a steady splat.
I travel on, a plodding pace,
I really feel like heck.
I brush the water from my face,
it's dripping down my neck.
Dripping, draining, from my hat,
it's dampening my shirt.
Pants seat wet, where I sat,
when I fell on slippery dirt;
pants legs, wet from dripping brush,
are stuffed in rain-filled boots.
We came out on this camping trip,
in the land of midnight sun.
I trudge on through the steady drip,
Now! we're having fun.

PART I
THE EARLY YEARS

Who can have more of this kind of fun than the cheechakos, the newcomers to Alaska? The next story will give you some idea of the adaptation to be made.

Like the majority of Alaskans, I came from some-where else...a cheechako, too. And, also like many of us, I was sent by the military, loved it here, and stayed.Learning to survive in this beautiful,but sometimes harsh,wilderness is an unforgettable experience for each of us.

COMING TO ALASKA

Twenty-six years ago, my uncle gave me some-thing — Uncle Sam, that is. It was a two-year, all expenses, paid trip to Fairbanks, Alaska.

Having always thought that I wanted to see Alaska, I didn't protest.That is, not until I arrived and discovered that the camp activity director's first planned event was a camping trip...in March...at thirty-five below zero. My blood, thinned by the training camps of Alabama and Georgia, ran cold.

"Aw geeze, Sarge," I said.

The activity director skewered me with an evil eye. I gulped, and shut up, resigned to being a happy camper.

My blood was to run much colder. At thirty-five below zero, all that fantastic cold weather gear is not much good. Oh, it keeps you from freezing completely to death, but you are constantly cold. Those tents are not exactly exotic hot houses either. And the "mummy bags", as their sleeping bags are called, may be fine for mummies...after all, mummies are already dead, and not concerned with conserving body heat.

I did fall in love with the military bunny boots. They are a must in Alaska, and I have never been without a pair since. On occasion, I have cleverly managed to get into overflow and fill my boots with ice water. After traveling back to my cabin, I have pulled the bunny boots off my perfectly warm feet, and poured out steaming water...heated to body temperature.

Those who survived the camping trip (Uncle Sam's activity director called it "an orientation"), were rewarded – with a pass to go to town. Actually, we all survived to get the pass. It only seemed that we wouldn't. Some of us may even have hoped we wouldn't.

I ran out to start my Chevy, driven up from

Georgia. Imagine my surprise. Thick, stateside axle grease had frozen stiff. In addition, the transmission would not shift out of second. As the engine turned over, the truck crept forward down the street.

The truck did not start, and the engine did not turn over for long, nothing else having been winterized. Oh well, isn't the hard way the only way to learn? My uncle had a very chilly olive drab bus that I rode to town. I was to ride it for the next month. At long last, spring came.

When it came to welcoming me to Alaska, Mother Nature pulled out all the stops.

After a bitter March and chilly April, she lulled me into complacency with a gorgeous, golden spring, of the sort Alaska is known for. Alas, it was not to last. This was 1967. In July, the earth quaked, mightily. As after-shocks continued, the skies opened up, and it rained...and rained...and rained some more.

The rivers rose, and in August the Chena River flowed over its banks and in my front door. The Tanana River added another couple feet on top...and the ground continued to shake.

My Chevy, by now carefully converted to an Alaskan rig, disappeared under several feet of water. It was, of course, a total loss. Another bitter winter was soon to follow.

Now, twenty-six years later, here I am — still in

Interior Alaska. Why? Hmm, it is a question I ask myself at times.

During our golden summers, with long, hot days of boating under twenty-four hours a day of golden sun and the fishing and hunting, or during the first months of lovely, delicate, fluffy snow, it's easy;"I love this place," I say.

Then comes January. It has been fifty below, or so, for four weeks, and is forecast to stay that way. Ice fog, thick and oppressive, hangs in the dark sky ...dark for twenty hours a day. The repulsive snow has long since ceased to be charming, or lovely. And it's much too cold for skiing, snow machining or ice fishing.

You love it here? Come on, Ted, get real!

Yet, there is a certain pride we take in being tough ones, a little hardier than most other Americans. That is part of the Alaskan mystique. Or are we a little fool-hardier than most?

I am reminded of the old joke about the man who was asked, "Why are you hitting yourself on the head with a hammer?" He replied, "Because it feels so good when I stop." (caution, kids, don't try this at home)

Perhaps that is why we endure our seven months of winter. By contrast, the summer is so wonderful. It feels so good.

THE PREMARITAL TEST

When I first met Plum, many years ago, she was the bookkeeper for Ed Burlison's Yukon Service, Inc., a local contractor.

Recently discharged by the Army, I was the accountant hired to audit the books. In those days, I was an imaginative young accountant and enjoyed checking out the bookkeepers' figures. I checked out Plum's and decided that it definitely would do.

We developed a friendly working relationship, laughing and joking, but I was a little shy...afraid to ask her out. One day, she took matters into her own hands and asked me to go on a snow machine trip with her and her friends to their cabin on the Salcha River. She had two snow machines, Arctic Cat Panthers, and I could use one, she said.

I jumped at the opportunity. A chance to get out in the Alaskan bush was something I had been longing for. Well, yes, I was longing for a chance to go out with her, too. Dottie, I called her in those days. That was before she became Plum, short for sugar plum, the wife.

The overland trip up the old mining trail was a joy. There was a well packed base with fresh powder snow on the trail, yet not too deep. The sky was clear and held a golden sun. At about zero, the temperature was pleasant, for snow -machining.

I loved it and the weekend at the cabin. We did a little riding, shot a few grouse for dinner, played a little cribbage (which, I was to learn, is the national game here). And I had a good chance to visit with and get to know people who are still our friends today.

In the course of the discussion, I discovered Plum not only had the two snow machines but she also had an airboat. On top of that, she had five acres of river front property on the Salcha. They pointed out the nicely timbered property to me. It looked like the perfect cabin site. This woman was looking better and better.

And she could cook, too! The grouse were delicious, simmered in barbeque sauce and served over rice. Little did I know the hazards –I have gained seventy pounds since I married her. It's all her fault, of course!

Sunday came. Time to head back to town. The temperature was minus forty-eight. At that temperature, snow machines do not run at their peak and we had problems with some of them. As a result, we ended up taking six hours to reach the highway.

The trip was only thirty-five miles, which gives you some idea of the problems. I will spare you the details. By then, I was too numb to shiver and I didn't get warm enough to shiver until I had spent several hours indoors. My frostbitten nose turned brown and wrinkled up. It looked somewhat like a rotten apple.

But next weekend, when she asked me again, I was enthusiastically ready to go. I had found my lifestyle. Plum later confided in me that I had passed her premarital test. For the river lifestyle is important to her.

I guess it was a good test. We have made it twenty years, so far. Though she still tests me, from time to time; tests my patience, if you know what I mean.

So we settled into a married life centered around the Salcha River and I began to break in to Alaskan activities...like boating.

Let me say right off, the Salcha is no river for a novice to break in on. The slow and gentle Chena that flows through Fairbanks is a much better choice for that purpose.

I, knowing no better, broke in on the Salcha river...really broke in (stove in the side of the boat – several times) broke the bottom, blew up the engine...times we would as soon forget).

My very first trip was at the steering wheel of an unfamiliar, flat bottomed, plywood airboat that Plum owned when we were married. I called her Sweetheart or Sugar Plum then – we were still on our honeymoon.

At the landing, I loaded Plum and my new mother-in-law, who had arrived in town just the night before, into the boat. Wide open went the throttle and we screamed off up river...actually made it half way up, too. Not bad for a beginner.

Suddenly, a stump loomed up, its roots embedded in the gravel river bottom. Obviously, it had heard me coming and sneakily jumped right out into the middle of the channel. I saw it too late!

Following the splintering crash, which dumped over my mother-in-law's chair, throwing her to the deck, we almost made it to shore before sinking in two feet of water. The hole in the side was large enough to stuff a six inch stove pipe through, but I hadn't planned on installing a galley.

River residents, Butch and Mary Hayes, rescued us (as they rescued so many others over the years), put us up for the night, then helped us patch the hole so that we could travel on.

Butch gruffly pointed out that there were intermediate positions on the throttle. I was amazed! My first boating lesson was learned, the hard way — but then that's how I usually learn.

Luckily, my mother-in-law has always been a good sport. She even still seems to like me.

GETTING HIGH IN ALASKA

In Alaska, I soon found, getting there really is half the fun. Since we have almost no roads, most of the state is accessible only by boat, snow -machine or airplane. Either way can make for a very interesting ride...and offer ever changing views of wild country and animals.

I'll never forget my first ride with a bush pilot. He had been recommended to me by a "friend". Ha! As the saying goes: with friends like this, who needs enemies? At least, that was my first impression.

Plum and I drove down the dusty, dirt road to the end, and stopped. Timidly, I peered about, wondering if we had come to the right place – or if this was a junk yard that we had wandered into by mistake. By the look on Plum's face, I could see that she was entertaining similar doubts.

All the remnants of airplanes littering the place did nothing for my confidence in the pilot or his craft. Some of them looked as though they had come to a bad end. The scattered remains included crushed noses, wings that had been literally torn off, and a fuselage twisted and blackened by some past fire.

Shakily, I recalled the pilot's nickname, "Crash". I had considered it to be an affectionate nickname, bestowed in jest by his friends. Now, I prayed that I had been right.

Just as I got out of my old Ford pickup truck, to

nervously scout for any signs of life, a remarkable character emerged from the tangle of junk. His face was wreathed by a cloud of whiskers, that I will swear had never known razor or shears, and topped by a second World War Aussie Digger's hat. The old set of Carhart coveralls he wore appeared to be held together only by the duct tape liberally wound around them.

"You the one who called about a flight out to the lake?" he asked. He spat chewing tobacco juice in a brown arc. Lucky for me that I was quick on my feet, only a little got on my left boot toe.

With considerable trepidation, I confessed that I was, indeed the one. "But where's your plane?" I asked.

"Right there," he pointed.

I could hardly believe my eyes, or ears. He was pointing at one of the wrecks. I could see that some-one had patched the tears in the fabric with yards of duct tape, but it looked like that was all that held the plane together. Studying it more closely I noted, with relief, that it was reinforced, here and there, with stout looking strands of mechanics' wire.

If it weren't for duct tape and mechanics' wire, civilization would long ago have come to an end in Alaska. Not only do we use it to patch parkas, coveralls and airplanes, but I personally have used duct tape to tape up cardboard boxes, to be used as suitcases, and find that it does reasonable service as a field expedient repair for plumbing or for radiator hoses.

One time I even used it for medical purposes. My friend Roger Redfern and I were out in the swamps of the Tanana flats, skinning out a nice bull moose, when he slipped and poked the tip of his Rapala knife right into the artery of his left wrist. Pretty, purple blood was squirting everywhere. Not having any other medical supplies, I duct taped the puncture on his wrist pretty tight and it held the blood flow until it clotted. I still think it was a sneaky way for him to get out of some work, though.

But I digress. Turning my eyes to the pilot, I said, "Some of these planes look like they had a little problem."

"Oh," he said, "I buy 'em up for parts. Lots of good parts there." He pointed at a hulk that looked as though the only salvageable part might be, possibly, one of the landing wheels. "...But enough chit-chat, we best be going." He led the way to his plane and helped us in.

We seated ourselves amongst the moose hairs, wisps of straw and pools of dried moose blood. The interior was aromatic, to say the least.

The plane roared down the meadow, faster and faster, straight toward a tall stand of spruce. White knuckled, I gripped the sissy bars. Now we were going to die. My heart thundered. My mouth was dry, while my palms were wringing wet − isn't it strange how that works?

About thirty feet from the spruce, the plane suddenly took off -- straight up, it seemed. By some miracle, we were up and over the spruce, and went into a tight turn.

Looking back, we saw Plum holding up the ceiling with both hands.

Crash laughed. "You don't have to hold her up," he said, "She'll stay up by herself." And he dribbled brown juice into an empty pop can.

It was a good flight. I only feared for my life one other time. It was as we approached the meadow near the lake, apparently planning to land there. Suddenly a siren started to sound. "Ooooga, ooooga!"

"What does that mean?" I questioned, nonchalantly, "Kiss your _ _ _ goodby?" But it was only the stall warning, sounding because our air speed had dropped, as, of course, it had to in order to land.

That trip, and other trips to follow, taught us that first impressions are not necessarily correct. Especially, perhaps, in Alaska. A rough appearance may hide a highly skilled professional.

NOTE: This is a composite, almost true story, but "Crash" is not any one particular individual. The names in some of my stories are changed to protect the author.

FEAR OF FLYING

She climbed into the tiny plane,
helped up by the pilot's hand.
She feared her prayers had been in vain,
fright's clutch was an icy band.

Her belly tight with unspoken fright,
she gulped back the taste of bile.
The pilot saw her stricken face,
she gave him a sickly smile.

He throttled out, the engines roared,
with a lurch they began to move.
They gathered speed across the pond,
tight clenched fingers were growing sore.

The towering spruce loomed straight ahead,
she muttered a silent prayer,
convinced that she would soon be dead,
that her crashing end was near.

With a stomach gripping, jarring lurch,
the plane broke free at last.
She wished she'd spent more time in church,
and had a purer past.

Into the air at sixty degrees,
it seemed impossibly steep,
the plane leapt up and cleared the trees.
Her knuckles were snowy white.

The plane laid up on its side,
and went into a tight turn.
She lifted her hands up to the roof,
her stomach began to churn.

Her sheer will power held up the plane,
or so it seemed to her.

The pilot then glanced back and laughed,
"You needn't hold it up."
"I promise you, a solemn vow,
it will stay aloft by itself."

And so she became a seasoned flier,
who climbs in without fear.
And nonchalantly takes the flight in stride,
beaming with good cheer.

But if you watch her close, you'll see,
her lips moving in prayer.

MAROONED...A STORY WITH A MORAL

In this vast, roadless, wild country, the rivers are our highways. This tale carries a message to boaters.

It was summer, many years ago...The boat hummed smoothly along, past high banks covered with mighty spruce, past gravel bars, rolling back through their fringe of willows into forests of birch and cottonwood. Well, this isn't so hard, I thought...even though I am new to boating.

Dainty creeks and dark mysterious sloughs empty into the main channel of the river. Behind and above all are the hills, rolling up toward the mountain peaks of the upper river.

The sun shines golden in a deep blue sky, reflecting in golden ripples off the water.

Summer in Alaska. Ah, the seclusion. That last camp must have been twenty miles back. There may not be anyone at all upstream from here. I wish we had come prepared to camp, rather than just for the day. I wouldn't mind staying here.

Clang! Rackety, clang, clang, clang. The boat drops off plane and begins to drift downstream. A quick look at the rod, hanging out a brand new hole in the side of the block, makes diagnosis of the problem quite simple. You don't even have to be a rocket scientist to figure it out.

I recall my thoughts of just moments before, with a sneer. I think that I would mind staying here. Belatedly, the old saying comes to mind — Be careful what you wish for, you may get it.

Quick work with the anchor and rope, and a little wading, gets the boat tied up to the bank. I am sopping wet. Good job, bringing the anchor — I almost came without one. I shudder, eyeing the tangled sweepers just below. I see a vivid picture of the boat, upside down under the logs together with its drowned crew.

What now, Captain? That engine is going nowhere under its own power and it may be several days before anyone comes along. I know that floating downstream is out, a good way to lose the boat — as well as, perhaps, our lives.

The younger child starts to yowl. The older one is already busily trying to drown himself, perched precariously on a sweeper, a tree that hangs out over the deepest swiftest current. I grab him back and administer a swift swat. Now they both are crying — what an improvement! Plum glares sullenly. Something tells me that this is not going to be one of our better family outings.

"I sure am glad that I had you give the neighbors that note about where we were going, and when we would be back," I say, "Roger will look for us when we don't show up. We might have been here a long time otherwise."

Plum has a very funny look on her face..."You mean this note?" she says faintly, dragging it out of her pocket. A tear trickles down her cheek, then another. Fantastic! Now all three of them are crying. Rover, sensing Plum's mood, joins in with a low wailing moan.

To escape, I go rummage in the boat. I get out the watertight drum that Roger packed as a survival kit for us, glad that I got some help and advice from an experienced boater. Let's see, I'll need the hatchet, bucket and shovel too. Roger told me to keep them and that kit in the boat at all times. I'm glad I did.

Drifting into my Buffalo Bill mode, I scan the area with an eagle eye, and select a suitable camp site. Out on the older part of the gravel bar, it's high enough that the river would have to rise a good bit to wash us out. Still, being on gravel, it will be easier to control the fire. The roots of an old washed in tree, full of dirt, offer one wall for our camp — a wind break.

At the camp site, I dump out Roger's survival kit. "Let's see what we have here," I mutter. Glory be! Roger is a genius. Right there on top of it all — a sack of lollipops. I conceal the sack, after taking out two for immediate use. The sniveling brats quiet down, a stick protruding from each mouth.

I set Plum and the brats to gathering fire wood. A productive chore is a morale builder, I reassure them. (Besides, we need the fire wood.)

That drum holds a cornucopia of treasure. Cooking utensils, lighters and fluid, rope and tarps, collapsible fishing rod with hooks and reel, a big first aid kit, coffee, a small jar of honey, can after can of food...and, what's this? —a fifth of vodka (obviously for medicinal purposes only), toy trucks, a cribbage board and deck of cards complete the kit.

Nothing was in cardboard containers that could be ruined should water leak into the kit.

Later, I gaze meditatively into the fire and sigh with satisfaction, as I sip my coffee sweetened with honey. It was fun catching enough grayling for dinner.

The rain spatters on the roof of our snug shelter, as Plum deals out cards for our first hand of cribbage.

Oldest belts littlest with the red toy truck. There are tears and howls. Let Plum straighten it out. Surreptitiously, I sweeten my coffee with a generous slug of vodka — nerve medicine, you understand. She jams another lollipop in each little mouth. Peace.

Next day, a passing boat (there had been someone up river from us after all) stops to give us a tow in.

The sun shines golden in a deep blue sky, reflecting in golden ripples off the water. Summer in Alaska. My beautiful, angelic children laugh.

Even Plum smiles. It has turned out to have been an enjoyable, if impromptu, camping trip. If you don't believe me, ask Plum.

Oh, I forgot to tell you the moral of this story...What? Yes, I guess you're right — you don't have to be a rocket scientist to figure that out either.

TENT CAMPING CAN BE A REAL TRIP

In time, we built ourselves a cabin on Plum's riverfront property —and became dwellers in the Alaskan bush.

Often, thoughtful friends who are travelling up the Salcha River bring us last Sunday's paper. Now, last Sunday's paper is a real treat to a bush dweller. We sit right down, taking the rest of the day off, and pretend that it is Sunday. We do the whole ritual — coffee and pastry, while we slowly peruse the paper.

My favorite part of the Sunday paper is the funnies — after that, the Weekender. Once I have read all the rest, I savor the advertising sections.

As it happens, we got a Sunday paper yesterday. Plum and I sat right down to enjoy it.

My eyes fell upon an ad for camping gear. I always enjoy ads for hardware, tools, sporting goods and camping gear. Anyway, tents were advertised — 7 x 7, sleeps three — said the ad. I smirked. Three may be able to squeeze in, but I am certain that they are not going to sleep, unless, maybe, they are midgets.

Indeed, Plum and I sometimes find that even our king size bed, at 6 x 6, seems a little crowded for comfortable sleeping for two people. But, then, she thrashes around something awful. She claims it is me that thrashes, but you have to consider the source.

Coming back to tents, though, I have always noticed that the advertised sleeping capability is wildly optimistic. The novice camper, of course, has no way of knowing this until he has suffered through a week of elbows in the kidney, knees in the back, or smelly feet in the face.

Once you have gotten three adults crammed into a seven by seven tent, what do you do with the week's worth of food, clothing, and personal items? Leave it out in the rain? Soggy toilet paper is gross. I will leave to your imagination the unappetizing state of some food items when soaked.

There are other things about tents that may not be immediately obvious, but should be considered.

I recall, for instance, the fantastic sale price that Plum got on a tent, a few years back. She was so proud of it! We took it moose hunting, and put it up. It went up easily. At nine by nine, it was comfortable for the two of us. We were very pleased with it, although I did wonder about the little round hole in the floor.

Then it began to rain. In the middle of the night, pitch black, it was a downpour that would make Noah nervous. I woke soaking wet, water streaming down my face as it poured in every seam. Now we were having fun!

After a long, cold night, in the first gray light of

dawn, we found a little dry wood and got a fire going. While I sat snarling by the fire, I looked at the box the tent had come in. Closer inspection of the packaging revealed that this was an ice fishing tent. Logically, since it never rains when one is ice fishing, ice fishing tents are not water proof — at least this one wasn't. Plum made me take her home, back to the cabin.

Oh well, if I ever go ice fishing, I'll have the tent for it.

It's not only tents that inspire salesmen to wild optimism in estimating how many people can sleep in. How about boats? Sleeps six they say. Peering into the claustrophobic below decks, we see two twin-size mattresses arranged in a v shape. Maybe they mean it sleeps six, two at a time in three eight-hour shifts.

Then there are motor homes, sixteen feet long, sleeps eight (but only if they are very friendly). It might do for a weekend, but can you imagine a long trip, the growing friction, the rage, the bloodshed? I guess though, that it really is all in how you look at it. We still keep a condo for our trips to town. It sleeps forty-eight, if you don't mind sleeping under the table, or on a pad atop the breakfast bar, or perhaps in the tub, or along the hall.

TENTING TONIGHT

I saw the ad about the tent.
To me it sounded heaven sent.
Seven by seven, sleeps three, it said.
Never a doubt entered my head.

When my wife and I went camping out,
putting up that tent was quite a bout.
Connect each pole A to each part B,
hook the whole mess to center part C.

The sagging tent was looking bad,
not a bit like the ad.
A billowing, sagging, drooping mess,
but I said, "It'll do, I guess."

This whole time, rain was pouring down.
I really feared that we might drown.
Along one side, we let her sleeping bag lie,
next a week of food, to keep it dry.

Spare clothes and gear
were next inside;
we had to keep them fully dried.

Under the flap I peered to see,
and looked and found...no room for me.

PART II
SPRINGTIME IN ALASKA

Our Arctic winters are severe, lasting seven or eight months, with snowfall up to twelve feet. Temperatures always fall to minus fifty, some years to minus sixty...occasionally to a spell of minus eighty. Any sign of spring is greeted with a hysterical glee.

THE NURSERY STORY

Winter, here in Alaska's interior, is a long one and I grow hungry for a glimpse of green.By January each year, I'm already leafing longingly through seed catalogues and planning my first excursion to the nursery. After all, it's only a few more months until spring.

It will not be long before seed trays line my window sills, as I try to get a head start on growing season. Poor spindly seedlings will struggle awhile, then perish...to be replaced by new ones until transplanting season finally arrives. I'm lucky the veggie rights people don't get after me, Plum says. Plum dislikes the mess, but has long since given up in despair. Gardening is an uncontrollable urge for me.

Fresh picked garden vegetables are a real treat but the season for growing them, here in Interior Alaska, is very short – often only ninety days. Quick maturing vegetables are at a premium.

Fifteen years ago, or so, we heard about a new nursery, in the nearby town of North Pole, that sold plants and seeds that were specially selected for this climate. Plum and I set out to inspect their merchandise.

Because I appeared to be lost, although I vigorously denied it, Plum insisted upon stopping at a gas station to ask directions.

"Do you know where the nursery is?" Plum asked the attendant.

To our surprise, he replied, "It's right over there, in the basement of the Baptist church." He pointed across the street.

"That seems odd," I remarked.

Plum said, "It must be a fund raising activity of the church."

We entered the church, to be greeted by a pleasant young lady. She asked if she could help us, and we asked to see the plants in the nursery. With a smile and nod she turned, leading us down stairs.

As we neared the bottom of the stairs, the shrill din of many children at play reached our ears...and the light dawned.

After controlling our embarrassed laughter, we apologized to the secretary of the Baptist day care center, a nursery for children.

FRUITLESS TOIL

I bought two little apple trees
not much higher than my knees.
I carried them home with pride
to plant them by my cabin side.

There were visions in my mind's eye
of apple sauce and apple pie.
I tended them all summer long,
but Mother Nature did me wrong.

Each grew to be a healthy tree.
But one day I glanced out to see
a passing moose, without a care,
take one big bite and strip them bare.

Naught remained but two bare stems
of my ravished little gems.
Next time I vowed I'd have the sense,
to build myself a big high fence

THE RITES OF SPRING

On my deck, I fire up the charcoal barbecue. It is the heat of the day now, two P.M., and I darn well intend to get the good of it.

Grimly determined, I kick aside the seven inches of fresh snow and brush off my deck chair. The clouds have broken and the late March sun shines bright. Ah, spring time.

Plum looks dubiously at my outfit of swim suit, breakup boots and knitted stocking cap. "Are you sure you want to do this?" she asks, "It's only twenty-four degrees."

The wimpy woman is bundled up in insulated boots and snow machine suit, with a fur hat—and in the heat of the day. Disgusting. I admit the morning was a little crisp, but now...for a tough Alaskan like me...it is sunning time. We have to get it when we can.

"Of course, I do," I snarl, briskly rubbing on some sun tan lotion. Brisk rubbing helps keep you warm. Crouching over the flaming charcoal briquettes doesn't hurt, either, but one must do it casually, to avoid blowing the image.

"I really don't understand why we always have to burn up a perfectly good piece of meat," Plum complains.

Comments like that are best ignored, so I do.

"Ah," I say, stretching in the sun, "About time the weather improved."

I had just dug my boat out of the snow drift, gotten out the garden tools, and started my plants in the greenhouse. I do it every year, thinking that this year will be different. And, of course, I have filled out my ice pool tickets, the lottery on the time the Tanana River ice will break up, for mid-April, as usual.

Spreading out the coals, I put the meat on the grill, a nice rack of ribs, and spread it with sauce to be baked on.

A gust of wind whips snow from the spruce trees. From the sunny edge of the roof (now a blistering thirty-three degrees) a trickle of icy water runs down my back.

"Ooh!" I exclaim, moving briskly away. Catching Plum's eyes upon me, I force a laugh. "Ha, refreshing." I rub some more sun tanning oil on — briskly, of course — and lean casually over the grill. To check the meat, you understand.

Alerted to a problem by the smell of smoke, I quick-wittedly extinguish my flaming chest hair with a splash of cola.

I look at the grill. Hmm, the sauce seems to be frozen on top of the meat. Oh well, turn it over and squeeze some sauce, through the ice crystals in the neck of the bottle, onto the other side.

I lounge a bit longer in the gorgeous spring weather, as the meat sits soggily on the grill.

Inspecting the meat again, I find that the sauce on this side is now frozen. Oh well, it's stuck on the meat — frozen on, baked on, whatever works.

My hands and arms are an odd shade of blue.

Solictitiously, I look at Plum. The poor woman looks cold. I feel a surge of compassion. Perhaps, I tell myself, it is time to take pity on the weaker sex.

"Heh, heh, heh," I say, suppressing a shiver, "You look awfully cold, Plum. Maybe we should put this meat in the oven at four hundred, just to keep it warm, you understand, and go listen to the news before dinner."

In my mind's eye I picture the crackling stove in the living room. I smile at her hopefully. She nods. My stratagem has worked. Thank Heaven, otherwise the woman would never let me hear the end of it.

You know how women are.

PLUM COLD

I woke up one weekend last March, knowing that it was morning, time to get up. Grey light filtered into the room and lit a misshapen lump in the covers. I poked the lump, experimentally. It snarled!

Following the snarl, it complained, "I'm cold." The voice was Plum's...she must be in there somewhere and I knew that I had better do some-thing...fast. Plum hates to be cold and the cabin had that early morning chill that cabins get at this time of year, after a night of the stove being banked down to hold its fire. So, I sprang up.

A shriek burst, unbidden, from my lips, as the

tender soles of my feet came into brutal contact with the ice cold floor. But, bravely, I pulled on my robe and slippers, staggered into the living room and opened the dampers. By the time I returned from starting the coffee, the stove had begun to roar.

I flipped on the television, which we run off a battery powered invertor, and watched the morning news, while warming my backside at the stove.

News of the latest boycott made me chuckle. It reminded me of a letter I got from an acquaintance down in the states. An acquaintance who wishes, always, to appear politically correct.

He lamented that he would like to plan for a vacation this summer but that there was no acceptable place left for a politically correct person to go. Alaska and Canada are out because of the wolf control proposals. Colorado and Oregon are out because of the gay controversy. I could go on, but you get the idea... there seems to be no politically correct vacation spot left. Or, at least, none that anyone would want to vacation in. It may be that Outer Slobovia has not offended anyone's sensibilities this year.

I sure am glad that I'm incorrect and don't have those problems. Minding my own business seems to be a full time job, without taking on the burden of telling everybody in the rest of the world how to live. Too bad they won't reciprocate and just leave us alone.

I turned the news off in disgust and switched my thoughts to a more pleasant subject ... my plans for ice fishing in the spring sun.

By now, the room glowed with a cozy warmth. Through the window, I could see peach-colored wisps of cloud lining the horizon...the beginning of a gorgeous day.

Plum lurched into the room. She had been drawn out of her den by the warmth. The gurgling sound of coffee reached my ears, but I kept my eyes averted. It's better to wait until after the first cup of coffee to acknowledge her presence.

This is one of my favorite times of year. Cold, dark, dreary January and February have gone. The temperatures of fifty and sixty below zero are behind us for another year. Now the days are usually long and sunny and warmer. A   promise of spring is in the air and the people are stirring into activity. We have the excitement of the Yukon Quest and the Iditarod — thousand mile sled dog races — Nenana Days festivities celebrating the raising of the ice pool tripod... And, soon, it will be time to turn in our ice pool tickets.

The ice pool is another ritual of spring that we enjoy, Plum and I. For a two dollar ticket there is the chance of winning up to $250,000. It adds a certain zest to watching the progress of breakup. The odds are forty-three thousand two hundred to one (60 minutes times twenty-four hours times thirty days equals forty-three thousand two hundred possible choices). Far better odds than the Publisher's Clearing House or Reader's Digest contests. Of course, we don't hold our breath waiting for our ticket to win — after thirty days, we would be a little blue in the face.

Our usual technique is to get a batch of ice pool tickets in early March. We fill them out with our best guesses, turn them in, and sit back waiting to collect our winnings. Then, inevitably, as the early April deadline approaches, we convince ourselves that it is warmer than we anticipated (or colder, depending on the year). Having decided that it is warmer, we convince ourselves that our first tickets are marked with dates far too late in the spring. The only solution is to rush out and buy some more. It adds to the excitement of developing spring. We've been doing things this way for twenty years now.

We actually won, one year. In 1990 the ice went out April 24th at 5:19 P.M. We were saddened, for our ticket was on 5:18. Imagine our joy, when they announced that no one held a ticket for 5:19 and the tickets on 5:18 and 5:20 would share the prize.

Our twenty-seven thousand six hundred dollar share made true believers of us and there is no way we would miss making our bets on the ice. Yes...I'm sure we will continue to turn in a second batch of tickets. After all, we're too old dogs to learn new tricks.

THE CALL OF THE WILD
I roam among the arctic peaks,
along the bubbling icy creeks.
To all who ask I do declare,
"I seek the gold that's buried there."
And yet, if pressed, I would admit,
the lure of gold's not all of it —
for the greatest treasure in my esteem,
is precious days spent by the stream.

Spruce and birch, those lovely trees,
are blowing in the whisp'ring breeze.
Underneath, yellow tundra rose
wafts its perfume to my nose.
Lightning flash and grey skies chill,
cause my every sense to thrill.
And when the grey gives way to blue,
'neath the sun shining a golden hue,

Then I bask in its rays so mild,
thankful for my days in the wild.
I see caribou and moose at play,
and fox and mink and wolf so grey.
Oh grizzly bear, you shambling brute,
go away, don't make me shoot.
With grouse and jays the woods are rife,
and squirrels chat of their teeming life.

And in the night by my campfire's light,
orange and flickering, leaping, bright
I sit there warm, beside the fire,
and know I've found my heart's desire.

GOLD FEVER

We breathe in the call of the wild and gold fever with every breath of fresh, Alaskan air, for the mystique of gold permeates Alaska's culture.

Fairbanks and North Pole nestle in the midst of a vast wilderness. White settlement in this area, known as The Golden Heart of Alaska, began during 1902 when Felix Pedro struck gold and a passing trader's stern wheel river boat stopped at the new mines, founding the first general store. To this day, we celebrate gold mining with the week long summer Golden Days festival.

Plum (short for Sugar Plum, the wife) and I succumbed to gold fever a number of years ago. Our first season of prospecting, 1987, the ice had gone out on the lower river by the first of May. Not realizing that the ice in the high country may break up as much as two weeks later, we rushed up river with our good friends and partners in prospecting, Roger and Betty Redfern.

We were stopped by an immense ice jam, and pulled into a quiet back water.

That night, we lay in the tent on the edge of sleep. Betty was restless, for we were deep in the heart of grizzly bear country — and grizzly bears have a nasty disposition.

Suddenly, she woke the rest of us.

"Listen!" she exclaimed tensely, "What was that?"

We strained to hear. Faint crackling noises grew to loud reports, like gunshots — and distant rumbling grew to something like the roar of an approaching freight train.

Hastily, we crawled out of the sleeping bags and ran from the tent, as the grinding roar swelled. It was light out for during mid-May in Alaska it is light twenty-four hours a day.

A wall of broken river ice, stacked two or three high, rumbled around the corner, grinding and groaning as the pieces jostled one another. The water of the Salcha River rose rapidly and huge chunks of ice filled our back water, trapping us and the boat for a week.

We had learned our first prospecting lesson — don't rush the season in the high country. Although we have read books and I have taken courses, most of our lessons in prospecting have been learned the hard way.

Gold prospecting is a gamble. The excitement is always with us. The next pan of dirt may lead to the big strike, or it may be in the next creek, or over the next hill. Yet, most of the time, for most of us prospectors, the total weight of mosquitos fed with our life's blood exceeds the weight of gold found.

The would be prospector,who wants to prospect next summer, should start early...say, by February, or so. The summer season is too short for any of it to be wasted — and there are things to be done before heading out for the creeks.

It's important to know if the area you plan to prospect is state or federal land, since different regulations apply. Equally important, is the knowledge of precisely where other claims and prospecting sites have been staked. Panning on someone else's claim may be not only illegal but also unhealthy.

Excellent, detailed maps of any area that you may be interested in can be purchased from the Geophysical Institute on the Fairbanks campus of the University of Alaska. On them, information can be marked about state or federal status and about other claims filed. This information can be obtained from the Federal Bureau of Land Management and the Alaska Division of Mines, both located in the complex across Airport Road from Fred Meyers in Fairbanks.

Alaskan Prospectors and Geologists Supply (504 College Road in Fairbanks) is very helpful to beginning small miners, offering assorted books on prospecting techniques and basic equipment like gold pans, sluices, suction dredges, gold screws, et cetera. The University of Alaska book store also offers books on techniques.

Once mining equipment is chosen and acquired, it is necessary to plan carefully what supplies to take. As a general rule, it's better to take too much rather than too little. Good prospecting sites are often a long ways from the nearest store.

I remember well that first trip Plum and I made. I carried endless boxes and bags to the boat. . Finally, I complained, "It seems to me that I have loaded far more in the boat than we had laid out to go."

"Well, I just thought of a few other things," she said.

I said, "It looks to me like you have everything but the..." my jaw dropped, as she stepped out the door carrying — you guessed it — a small, chrome kitchen sink.

"It's only a little one," she said, defensively.

Prospecting has its hardships and its rewards. Many days are golden, a hot sun in a blue sky, clear pure water chuckling by, grayling, fresh from the creek to the pan, for dinner. Other days are harsh, cold and wet.

The harsh conditions, cold and wind, soakings from rain or from falling in the creek, and the keen appetite developed by hard work in the fresh air, yield a deep appreciation for the simple things of life. The crackling warmth of a wood fire, the inner glow from a hot cup of coffee, the comfort of crawling into a warm sleeping bag with a belly full of hash, the cleansing blast of a warm shower, all become luxuries to savor. This heightened appreciation of simple pleasures is part of the reward.

It is hard to describe the joy of knowing that there is no one for seventy miles, or more, in any direction. There is a precious sense of peace and freedom.

We have not found enough gold to set off another big stampede, or, even, to pay expenses. There is always hope of the big strike, but the prospecting experience is, indeed, a treasure in itself.

As a historical note, the largest nugget ever found in Alaska came out of Anvil Creek at Nome. It weighed 155 troy ounces and would be worth approximately $60,000 at today's prices, if melted down and sold...not a bad day's work, finding something like that.

We have always loved the Kenai Peninsula and Kachemak Bay. At least once a summer, we try to go clamming and halibut fishing in this beautiful setting.

KACHEMAK BAY - The fishing trip

(in the Gulf of Alaska)
At minus five, the tide is out,
a drop of thirty feet.
The floating docks lie far below,
the ramps seem awful steep.
I swallow hard, looking down,
I promised myself this treat.
Down the ramp I force myself,
onto the boat I leap.
Beyond the spit are rolling waves,
I force myself aboard.

The captain heard me mumbling,
a prayer to the Lord,
"I came out for the halibut,
not to go to my reward."
"The waves are not too bad," he said.
IIis smile conveyed good cheer.
Looking at the three foot swell,
I consoled me with a beer.
We bounced on out through rising seas;
for this I paid good cash?!

continued on next page

An hour or more away from shore,
the anchor made a splash.
I took the rod, the bait went down,
into the raging sea.
The rolling boat, the five foot waves,
up and down the bait,
In rising wind and rising sea,
breakfast deserted me.
And yet, and still, I felt a thrill,
a tug of a heavy weight.

I fought it in, with tired arms,
my rod was sharply bent.
A monstrous halibut came to gaff,
two hundred pounds he went.
Then we turned, and ran for shore,
through angry towering seas,
I puked and puked,
three hours or more,
and landed with wobbly knees.
But please take me back to Kachemak,
I want to go back for more.

JUST FOR THE HALIBUT

A few years ago, Plum and I headed south in mid-May, planning to break our trip with an overnight stay in Anchorage. The total trip would be about six hundred miles, half the length of Alaska, but road conditions make it a long, slow six hundred miles ...especially from Anchorage on south. We were headed for Homer and our first halibut charter. The trip to Anchorage was made through forests and over passes familiar to us. The route took us over a shoulder of mighty Mount Mckinley but the mountain was lost in the clouds.

Next day, our adventure took us into new territory. Leaving the south side of Anchorage, we drove on the Seward Highway out Turnagain Arm to Portage, where the road turned the corner on that end of the sea's arm and headed south down the Kenai Peninsula.

Although the day was overcast, with a light drizzle, as is so often the case in coastal areas, it was a beautiful drive. The highway climbed into the cloud-capped mountains and their beauty shone despite the overcast.

As we went over the top of the range and headed down, Plum gasped, nearly running off the road as she came upon our first view of the Kenai River, world famous for its king salmon fishing.

The clouds had broken and the river sparkled like

a jewel. The sight left her breathless and she pulled off the road to stare in absorbed admiration.

"Why hadn't I heard about the color? It's a vibrant turquoise green. What an incredible color for a river, vivid and beautiful! Yet no one ever has ever mentioned it," she said.

We took a lengthy break from driving and ate our lunch, caribou salad sandwiches, gazing at the Kenai River the whole time. Driving on, we found that the road wound along the Kenai, through Soldotna, to the coast of Cook Inlet. Each view of the river dazzled us, as it emerged.

We drove on south down the coast, past Clam Gulch, Clam Shell Lane, Clam Shovel Road, Razor Clam Drive and assorted other side roads named Clam this and Clam that.

"One might get the impression that they dig a lot of clams around here," Plum said, and chuckled.

Tired from the long drive, she pulled off onto a gravel area on top of a high cliff. Far below rolled the ocean.

Along the shores of the Cook Inlet, we could see the massive cones of several volcanoes, amongst them Mount Redoubt, topped with fire as a new eruption burst from its summit.

Near the end, the road started downhill. A panorama of sea and rugged mountains lay before us, with Homer Spit projecting out into Kachemak Bay and surrounded by a busy fleet of boats. Over two hundred halibut charter boats make their home port here, in addition to the commercial fishermen for halibut, salmon, crab, shrimp and other seafood.

I was to discover, later, that the residents call these charter boats "pukers"— and for a very good reason. (However, I found the prescription seasickness patches to be very effective for me).

Six A.M. the next day found us at the head of the harbor stairs — steep, open, ironwork grate ramps, actually.

Pausing, we looked out over the hundreds of boats moored far below. It was a picturesque sight. All sizes, shapes and colors of boats, and all different sorts of equipment.

Plum looked down through the ramp.

She gulped and exclaimed, "Oh! The ramp looks awfully steep and the water seems far below."

With her heels hooked into the rungs spaced down one side of the ramp, she clutched the hand rail tightly, with white knuckled hands, and began to work her way down. She held her breath as she approached the midsection of the ramp and I heard an audible sigh of relief, as she stepped off the ramp and onto the docks, thirty feet below the parking area.

We were to be very surprised, when we returned that afternoon, to find the docks at nearly the same level as the parking lot and the ramps level. The Cook Inlet tides can change nearly forty feet. It is something that must be seen, to be comprehended.

It is an incomparable way to spend a day — on the sea, amongst the looming mountains and ragged islands, each with its individual cap of cloud. The tang of fresh salt air mingles with the perfume of spruce blowing from the land. Sun glints golden across the water. The rhythmic thump of the lead on the bottom travels up the line. It is followed often by the pull of heavy weight and a surge of elation. Our trips have all featured constant action all day long, as we catch and release cod or smaller halibut and keep the larger ones.

And fresh caught halibut is a food for the gods...true ambrosia, either broiled or chunked, beer battered and fried. A halibut charter is a trip every man owes himself at least once before he dies.

FISH STORIES

Opening day on the Salcha River, the first Saturday in June, my mouth watered for the first grayling of the season. My fly settled lightly, to kiss the surface of the water, and floated high and free on the current, until the river exploded. A monstrous grayling took my Coachman, leaping clear out of the water. He must have been a twenty incher, or more.

Back and forth, he dashed, fighting all the way as I gathered in line. Closer and closer, almost at my feet. I could see him, half out of the shallow water along the gravel bar, the fly barely in his lip.

A quick surge forward gave him a little slack and the fly dropped loose. I was horrified...I really wanted that fish. Reflexes faster than thought, I belly flopped on him and felt wriggling all the way up my belly and tickling at my throat as he wriggled his way free and was gone. I also felt the thrill of ice cold water, lapping about me, and jumped up with a shriek.

Strange things can befall fishermen.

During July last year, I spent some time prospecting for gold on the Middle Fork of the Salcha River. The day I headed back down to my cabin, I poked along — panning a side creek a little here, looking for game signs there, and checking the ripeness of the blue berries another place. Just generally having a good time. I had my fly rod along.

As I went on down the main river, below the forks, I noticed a small plane flying up and down the river, sometimes circling. It seemed familiar, but I couldn't place it. When I happened upon my friend, Lefty (sometimes known as Lyin' Lefty), who was fishing along the bank, I pulled over, stopped, and asked whose plane it was.

He replied that it was Fish and Game, counting salmon, but, he told me, they couldn't see any and were planning on closing commercial, subsistence and sport fishing as a result.

The plane flew over again, at about a hundred feet. Hmmm, I looked into the water, swollen and brownish from heavy rains.

By golly, they were right, I couldn't see any salmon either — matter of fact, I couldn't see anything.

My hand disappeared into the murk, a few inches below the surface. I lowered my face until my glasses were just on the top of the water, still nothing. I stuck my face into the water — Oh No! I had gone blind. What a terrifying experience. In a panic I jerked back...and it was a miracle!...I could see again.

It seemed senseless, that they would try to spot salmon from an airplane in these conditions. But, then, I heard it from Lefty— who has been known to abuse the truth on occasion.

Anyway, muddy or not, I decided to try for a couple of grayling for dinner. I cast out, a silver number two Mepps spinner.

And what did I catch? A little pike, far too small to be a keeper. Carefully and considerately I eased the hook out of his little mouth, carefully avoiding the sharp baby teeth (pike are carnivorous). I'd throw him back to grow up, I thought. I returned him, oh so gently to the water. His sides heaved as he lay there, motionless. I stroked his back lightly with my finger— and he promptly turned belly up.

Oh no! I seized him, held him upright, and moved him gently back and forth to force water into his gills. I considered mouth to mouth resuscitation. Suddenly he revived, restored to life...he bit me, of course. Gosh, I never knew a fish that small could bite so hard.

Sometimes we catch grayling. Sometimes, when it's stormy or the water high and muddy, we catch none. Always, Plum and I have a good time trying. It is pure pleasure just being out on the crick.

MOUNTAIN STORM

A breath of breeze stirred the spruce;
it made the faintest sigh.
An ominous, greenish light,
grew in the western sky.

The rising wind's low pitched wail,
(I was uneasy and alone)
reminded me of the ancient tale,
of the banshee's sobbing moan.

The usual sounds of forest life,
of love and song and strife,
were silent now, nothing heard,
from squirrel, or moose, or bird.

The angry clouds were boiling black,
a purple hue behind.
At lightning's flash & thunder's crack,
I feared I'd lose my mind.

The rolling booms, the streaks of light
the shaking of the ground;
I feared I'd lost my ears and sight,
t'was so loud there was no sound.

And then the sun came creeping out,
the sky changed back to blue;
the birds were singing all about,
I saw the rainbow, too.

SPRING SOLSTICE
(June 21st)

A funny thing happened in my front yard yesterday morning, though I guess that calling it a yard may be pushing it, since it consists mostly of brush and weeds that I mow once every summer, along about mid-summer, whether it needs mowed or not.

Fly rod in hand, I was moseying along the front bank, prospecting for breakfast. A couple of decent sized grayling was what I had in mind.

Pretty soon, I had one rising to the fly. He was just a little further out than where my cast was settling. So, I worked out a little more line before casting again. Wham! The line pulled tight, against a hook that was obviously firmly set... too bad that it was set behind me.

I had a problem. Plum's shriek alerted me to the fact. I surveyed the situation with considerable apprehension. What a relief, to see my Royal Coachman merely hooked in her bathing suit strap, not in some tender portion of Plum's anatomy. I had feared that I would have to cut the barb off the hook to get it out of her and I prize my Coachmen. Good fishing flies are expensive, skin grows back... as I have often assured Plum.

I did a double take at the swim suit. It was warm out. So warm that Plum had actually taken off her bunny boots and snowmachine suit and even her fur hat.

A low whistle escaped me...nice swimsuit! I had forgotten during our eight month winter...But wait, Plum is notoriously cold blooded. Why, it's even rumored that she has worn a sweat suit at Waikiki. My heart sank...we must be headed for a melt down.

But yesterday was the day of the solstice, longest day of the year, and it did get hot.

While I stood there, wearing a silly grin, Plum's scowl had grown threatening, even frightening. Hastily, I began working on getting the hook out of her suit. Meantime I sought to divert her with a tale.

"That was quite a shock," I said, "when the hook set behind me. Reminded me all too vividly of the time, the same thing happened and I turned around to find a grizzly bear on the other end of the line. The hook was in his mouth, too, though I suppose that was a coincidence."

"What happened?" Plum gasped.

"Aw," I said, regretfully, "he broke the line and got away."

Plum's eyes grew enormous.

As you may have previously gathered, Plum is one to take things a little too literally. I'll never forget the time, some years ago...We were having a little dispute with the I.R.S. ...And then she got the letter from them marked 'FINAL NOTICE'. "Oh, good," she said, "That means we won't be getting any more letters from those nasty people."

Her belief in the grizzly bear story lasted only a moment though — I couldn't keep a straight face — and she stormed off in a huff.

Anyway, the solstice has come, the end of a long winter.

But what's this? Plum is breaking out her long johns again. She tells me that tomorrow we start losing daylight — headed back into winter. What a cheerful thought! Anyone for Hawaii?

PART III
GOLDEN ARCTIC SUMMER

Golden, glowing, midnight sun slides along the northern horizon...to rise again in the north - east. Twenty-four hour a day of sunlight and temperatures reaching into the eighties and nineties above zero, fahrenheit, stir the land to life. Plants grow explosively, with cabbages reaching several hundred pounds weight in ninety days. The fish are biting, the living is easy.

THE SPORTSMAN'S ART

A major factor in our food supply and a central part of our life style and culture is fishing and hunting.

The other day, I was frying up a mess of french fries and beer battered chunks of caribou sirloin. As I sat out on my deck, watching the grease bubble in the pot, a nice little bull moose strolled through the yard. The sight turned my thoughts to hunting, and my hearty enjoyment of the outdoors.

I reminisced about hunting seasons past — and about the many sportsman's skills I have acquired over the years.

A true sportsman must learn a number of skills: fire building, camping, accurate shooting, fly casting, and many others. But to be truly recognized by his fellows as a mature and seasoned sportsman, he must master the art of gentle prevarication.

Plum is reading this over my shoulder. "Prevarication?...Lying, you mean," she shrills indignantly.

Plum just doesn't appreciate the subtle nuances, the skill, required of a master prevaricator. At least, she didn't, but there was one occasion...I remember it well.

On that particular occasion, we had gotten a moose with a very nice rack. She was very proud of it. Next day, with the moose hung at the cabin and cared for, we were out fishing when Lyin' Lefty stopped at the bank.

Lefty had a nice moose in his boat, the rack prominently displayed on the bow. He beamed with pride. "Look here," he boasted, "a sixty-one incher." His was much smaller than ours, of course. I thought to myself, 'They are forty-eight inchers, if I ever saw any.'

Plum and I looked at each other. I saw that odd way she has of rolling her eyes and pursing her lips when she detects a failed prevarication.

Hastily, I cut her off. "Very nice moose, Lefty," I said, "Did you measure from here to here." I indicated straight across at the widest point.

"Oh no," he replied, "the proper way to measure horns is on the diagonal, whichever way gives the biggest measurement." He gestured, from top left to bottom right of the rack.

We accepted that politely, for the moment, though I could see Plum's eyes rolling dangerously. Now, I'm not one to hurt a person's feelings by calling "B— S—!" Besides, at times I fear that I would lose my voice if I called "B— S—!" every time I heard it.

Lefty naively chattered on a few moments...he doesn't recognize the signs. But soon, he moved on down stream.

As he disappeared around the corner, Plum cried out in wrath, "Sixty-one inches! If those horns are sixty-one inches, ours must be at least ninety." Her eyes were flashing with temper.

We raced back to the cabin and I whipped out my pocket tape measure, wrapped it around the horns a couple of times, and exclaimed triumphantly "One hundred twenty-two inches! What a monster!"

I was excited — and grateful to Lyin' Lefty for explaining how it was done. He had qualities that I had not fully appreciated before. It just goes to show how we all can learn something new, even an old hand like me.

Plum wore an odd new expression, a smile lingered on her lips. "He did say that the proper way was to measure however you get the biggest measurement," she murmured softly.

She was beginning to appreciate the fine art of gentle prevarication.

Maybe there is hope, yet, that she will become a mature and seasoned sportsman. Why, not long ago, we were out ice fishing, and I noticed her surreptitiously double up the tape to measure her fish, when she thought I wasn't looking — Just because we had a bet on who would get the biggest fish...the loser to wash the dinner dishes.

"A thirty-six inch grayling," she shouted.

For shame, Sugar Plum!

THE ONE THAT GOT AWAY
While driving up the highway,
I saw a mighty moose,
dribbling globs of pond weed,
like trapper Ron dribbles snoose.
Now I was up near Cantwell,
on my way home from the fair.
And though I hate to say it,
my freezer was mighty bare.
"What's the season? What's the rules?"
I rummaged out the book.
The big bull stood there patient,
while I took a hasty look.
And in the book I sadly read,
"The rack must be fifty-five inches
or more across its spread...
or you must leave the moose alive.
Fifty-four? or fifty-six? So ran my mind's debate.
My mental tape ran round his rack...
Hell! — He'd easy go fifty-<u>eight</u>!
I pulled my rifle to my shoulder.
I had him in my sight.
The knuckle on my finger turned a snowy white.
But then I held my fire,recalling how the mind
can grow antlers on the brow
of a thoroughly bare-headed,
luscious looking... <u>cow</u>.
And as I thought, anxiety fraught,
he took a step, then two.
And vanished in the concealing brush.

And then my hunt was through.

LYIN' LEFTY'S MOOSE

Like fishermen, the hunters, too,
are known for tales that aren't quite true.
Of them all, Lyin' Lefty's are worst.
And he tells each one unrehearsed —
quite impromptu, if you will,
like the day he boasted a fresh kill.

"I killed it with one shot," he said.
"A single shot left it lying dead."
His partner spluttered in amaze,
giving him an unbelieving gaze,
and said, "Don't you find it quite uncouth,
to utter such a bold untruth."

"You emptied out your gun,
and missed with every one —
but the last, which knocked him dead,
with a lucky shot to the head."
Lefty capered about with glee
and chortled, "There, now you see."

"I killed it with a single shot.
whether you believe it, or not."
Put that way, I had to agree,
"One shot is all it ever takes me...
The last, of course," I said with a frown,
"Why keep on shooting, once he's down."

A WAY OF LIFE - A WAY OF LOVE
(evolution of an Alaskan soul)

The boy trudged through the creek bottom, warmly aware of the brightness and tangy scent of the golden autumn leaves. To his left, the little creek chuckled and splashed.

The seven year old treasured the smooth feeling metal barrels and polished wood stock of the twenty-eight gauge shotgun he had been trusted with. He also treasured the silent companionship of the big man who walked beside him.

Suddenly, the brush erupted with a drum-like rumble and a burst of motion. A brown streak burst into flight and the boy's heart leapt into his throat. Adrenaline-driven blood surged hotly through his veins, as he thumbed back a hammer and raised the shotgun to his shoulder. He tracked the ruffled grouse with the barrel and the gun popped. The bird dropped to the forest floor.

"Nice shot," he heard. The man's hand rested on his head, conveying approval and love. His first grouse...a landmark event. All that practice had paid off. The pleasant scent of burnt powder tantalized his nostrils.

That evening, as they returned home with enough grouse for dinner and a bucket of wild elderberries for pie, the boy strutted a little — he was bringing home the evening meal for his family.

That boy was me. The man was my Dad. Over the years, we spent many a happy hour in the woods of Montana hunting grouse and deer, fishing for trout, gathering berries. It was a central part of our lifestyle — the important part...And wild foods were an important part of our diet.

Now, this year, I turned fifty. Together with Plum, I have been wandering the forests of Interior Alaska for twenty-six years. Long, golden days, spent on the rivers and swamps, have enriched our marriage. In the peace of the forest we share silent, contemplative companionship or lively conversation. Problems get solved and plans made...articles get written or the next novel planned.

As a bonus of our hunting and gathering, our family eats healthier food. Game meat is low in fat and cholesterol, without any of the chemicals that lurk as residues in commercial meats. And it is delicious when properly prepared.

We have raised our two children, mostly on moose, caribou and grayling, and they have gone out into the world and have children of their own. Now, all we want is to continue our lifestyle in peace and freedom — and to preserve the option of living this lifestyle for our grandchildren. We are, in short, typical of many long-term residents of Alaska.

Nearing fifty, a belief in my own mortality established itself. I had wasted too much precious time in business, I decided, with only weekends in the wilds — so I sold my accounting practice, a few years ago, and turned my attention to personal fulfillment. The following poem was written about that time.

MIDLIFE

Many years once lay ahead,
an endless treasure it seemed.
Fifty now, I'm filled with dread.
What became of all I dreamed?

Where did that endless treasure go?
Did I mush those huskies across the snow?
Dig for gold with my bare hands?
Explore exotic tropic sands?

Did I write a book, craft a verse?
No!

They slip by so fast, those precious years,
forever gone, too late for tears.
But it's not too late, a few remain.
I'll see tropic seas and France and Spain.

I'll waste no more, I'll write my book,
and song and verse, and dig for gold.
And when, at last, my tale is told,
no regrets -- I will have lived my dreams.

TEACHING THE KIDS TO FISH

Teaching the kids to fish — it's a joy, a challenge, a hazardous duty. A dad or grandpa can develop an odd looking twitch, flinching from the shadows of passing birds, the sound of a fluttering flag, any peripherally perceived motion.

Though it may look strange, this twitching is preferable to the alternative...barbed hooks hanging from the flesh of a too slow dad. Grandpas are less likely to suffer this indignity, since the twitch is a skill like riding a bike — once learned, it's never forgotten.

My son Mark, when first learning to fish, had trouble getting a light, number two MEPPS spinner to cast out far enough. So, one day, I put on a heavy, number four MEPPS for him. He wound up and cast mightily, though inaccurately.

The hollow thump of the heavy spoon, colliding with the back of Mark's head, reminded me of the time I dropped a luscious, ripe watermelon on the sidewalk. Of course, the goose egg was enormous. Equally of course, I was in big trouble with Plum.

The real fancy dodging, on my part, came when I began to teach Mark and daughter Amy fly fishing. The whistle of a sharp pointed fly, whipping by your ear, is guaranteed to get your immediate attention. And these whistling flies can cover a considerable, quite random area, too.

Kids have a natural affinity for water, regardless of how cold the day or how they are dressed. As a young parent, you worry about that: "If you kids get your feet and pants wet one more time, you're really going to get it." Or, sometimes, "Next time you are really going to get it." They never questioned what they were going to get, probably because of the mood of those moments. Good thing, because I didn't know what they were going to get either.

In any case, grandparents are much more relaxed, having found out that kids are pretty tough...they don't dissolve in the rain or in river water — and seem to recover nicely from the inevitable series of scrapes and bruises. The grandson can get his feet wet...or his whole body — clothes and all — without it being a catastrophe.

Teaching the kids to fish carries its own reward...the excitement, joy and pride of a young angler making his or her first catches.

All the associated talents come easy to them. My grandson Nick recently caught his first fish — all by himself... the first fish caught that day...and the largest fish of the day, a nice eighteen inch grayling. At the landing, we met a friend, Paul Quakenbush, who asked how big Nick's fish was. "Bigger than mine?" Paul teased, holding his hands about 24 inches apart. Nick nodded, his hands automatically springing up to a position about 30 inches apart. It must be in the genes, the talent for prevarication.

AUGUST CARIBOU

Many contend that a hunting partner should be hairy faced and ugly. Not mine! For those who haven't tried taking their wife or girl friend hunting (as a hunting partner, not the camp cook and dish washer), I highly recommend it.

I recall a trip, for example...It was opening day...eight o'clock in the evening, the sun shone hot and golden in a deep blue sky. It doesn't get dark in Interior Alaska until nearly eleven at this time of year. We were in the high country on the Middle Fork of the Salcha River, one hundred twenty miles from the highway. It had been a long but pleasant day, hunting all the way up river to here.

Plum, our close friend Betty Redfern and I had just gotten set up in camp, and relaxed in the sun, roasting hot dogs and marshmallows over an open fire.

What a tranquil, relaxing time. The birds were singing, a squirrel chirped. We were happy. It doesn't get better than this.

Suddenly, Betty exclaimed, "What's that?... Listen!"

Listening intently, we heard a 'clop, clop, clop splash, splash'. Holy smoke! It sounded just like the sound track of an old western — the part where the bad guys are riding up the creek on their horses.

A massive animal burst into view, running down the shallows. An enormous spread of horns flashed at us.

"It's a moose!" I yelled, at first glimpse.

"No, it's a bull caribou!"Betty cried, excitedly, " A huge one ." We had not anticipated an animal coming right into camp, with a fire burning and all, and we didn't have a rifle handy. The plan had been to get ready for the morning hunt after dinner. (Is there a moral to this story?)

Hot dogs and marshmallows ended up in the flames, sticks and all. Dinner burned up, unnoticed, as we scrambled for our rifles.

During the commotion, the big bull disappeared around the bend, leaving us red faced, but with rifles in hand. I grasped mine firmly.

My heart thundered, as I took off running down the gravel bar and burst through the willow brush, to see the bull standing in plain sight several hundred yards down stream.

He ambled into the brush, just as the ladies arrived on the scene, breathless from their run. We got the boat and went down stream to the spot.

I tied up the boat about where I had last seen him. Where was he? I wondered. This was a real thicket. We set out to search.

A loud whoof burst from the bull as he sensed my presence and turned, his massive horns rising above the brush twenty feet or so from me.

My heart stopped. He had me, I knew it, but he didn't charge. My rifle leapt up, almost of its own accord, and fired a round through his head.

As we admired our meat, before setting to work dressing it out, a huge grizzly slunk across the bar down stream from us, looking every bit like a cat stalking a bird. He slithered into the river and swam to our side.

Shaken, and knowing dark would be coming on, we put Betty and her magnum on bear guard while we hastily field dressed the caribou. Luckily, the bear never came then, though the gut pile was gone next day.

Next morning, sight of the quarters and rack hanging in the trees behind our camp had us all charged up to go after the rest of our winter meat. We made a morning run.

It was a crisp morning, a hint of frost already in the air in this high country.

We ran for an hour or so, seeing nothing — except lots of beautiful country. It was another clear day, golden sun in a pure, blue sky. A wonderful day and place to be alive.

Then it was time for breakfast. We broke out our fishing poles, and cast, letting our flies settle lightly to kiss the surface of the river. Each of us had breakfast on the hook in seconds, lively, colorful Arctic grayling.

Upper Salcha is our favorite hunting ground, for it offers outstanding mixed bag potential: caribou, moose, grayling, black and grizzly bears, and grouse. Although we haven't hunted them, we have seen an occasional sheep.

Over a drift wood fire, we soon had sizzling pans of cooking bacon, fish and fried potatoes. A thermos yielded coffee, with a generous splash of Irish Cream in it, to round out the meal.

Happily stuffed, we set off hunting again. Within fifteen minutes or so, we came to a long, curving gravel bar.

There, about a hundred yards up the bar, were three caribou, at the bar for a little sociable drink — a bull session, if you will.

Two of them were nice sized bulls. I ran up to the bar with the boat, and shut off the engine, letting the boat settle to rest on the gravel.

The ladies executed a couple of very nice head shots, bringing both bulls down on the edge of the gravel, a short way apart.

Betty's husband, Roger, was unable to come with us that trip. As dealer for Alumitech airboats, hunting season is a busy time for him, checking and tuning up boats, repairing damaged boats and getting new boats ready.

He was delighted with our boat full of August caribou. Often, it is the ladies and I, or Plum and I, who hunt together, most enjoyably, for my lady gunners are the best hunting partners a man could ask for.

Hunting together is something that Plum and I both eagerly anticipate, one of the high spots of the year. The shared experience out in the beauties of Alaska's wilds strengthens our relationship.

Some unsuccessful male hunters, ego wounded, have complained about the ladies' luck. Hunting, they say, is a man's occupation.

I enjoyed the perfect squelch that a friend on the river came up with. "Well, Sir," he said to the complainer, "maybe if you got you some panties and a bra, you could get some game, too."

TO CATCH A BEAR

Based on our experiences during another hunt, the ladies and I have concluded that the very best way to catch a bear is to buy an ice chest — a very expensive ice chest, since bears are discriminating about the quality of ice chest they tear up.

Next, load the ice chest with things that you especially enjoy eating — like smoked ham, smoked salmon, cold fried chicken... you get the picture. Go out to the woods, set up camp, and sit down to eat dinner...opening the ice chest frequently to extract food items and eat them with obvious enjoyment. This tough duty is, of course, a show for the bears that are peering at you from the surrounding brush. After a time, lie down and pretend to sleep.

The story of another of our August caribou hunting trips is illustrative:

"Look at this!" I hollered to Plum, I pointed down. "Someone has dropped a blueberry pie beside the trail...recently, too, it's still steaming."

"Old fool," she said, grinning, "You know darn well that's bear poop."

Betty Redfern, pointed out the nearby tracks, again, very fresh looking (the tracks, I mean, not Betty).

We didn't let that deter us, though; bears are a fact of life here. We went on about our business of packing gear from the boat to the campsite.

The bear was forgotten, until that evening. Betty, Plum and I had settled into our sleeping bags, snuggling gratefully into the warmth, for the night air gets cool at this time of year.

Our eyes had just dropped shut and I heard the first snores...probably Plum, I concluded, though she insists that it is me that snores. Come to think of it, maybe it was Betty snoring! Suddenly, a slamming sound jerked me erect...the sound of an ice chest lid, slamming shut.

A fine looking black bear edged guiltily away from the edge of the clearing, dropping the pound of butter he held; a few bites were missing. That bear looked huge...like, maybe, eight hundred pounds, there in the twilight.

We, of course grabbed our rifles, visions of juicy bear steaks dancing in our heads. A black streak blurred into the distance, before my rifle reached my shoulder. Never have seen an animal move so fast.

Our hunters' blood ran hot and, thinking that it may have stopped after a short distance, we sprang up and pursued.

A few minutes later, I found myself and the two girls running barefoot and in long johns across the mossy forest ...chasing a bear through the gathering dusk.

"Halt," I screeched...and we did. Reason returned, this was not too bright.

A short time later, back in camp, we settled in for the night.

Next morning, I woke to see the bear skulking at the edge of the clearing... eating the rest of the butter, the memory of which had obviously been troubling her all night. A quick shot brought her down and we had a start on our winter meat. Funny though, in the daylight that 800 pound bear shrank to only about 150 pounds. Perceptions can play strange tricks.

THE BEAR FACTS

Black bears are delicious, so long as they haven't been gorging on dead salmon or the local garbage dump. Their flesh is flavored by what they eat. By September the peak salmon runs are over and most black bears in the forest have changed their diet from rotting salmon to berries: blue berries, bear berries, cranberries; and their flesh is sweet and good, rather like pork in texture and flavor.

These bears eat nearly anything — but a good place to find them is around good berry patches or feeding on gut piles where other game has been field dressed. They are a major menace to moose and caribou populations...especially in the spring, when they kill heavily pregnant cows in order to tear out and eat the uterus and unborn calf. Awkward new born calves are also easy prey; less than 20 percent of them surviving the depredations of wolves and bears to reach one year of age.

Proper identification of the species of bear is important, since there are very stern restrictions and limitations on harvesting grizzlies (and a special tag is required). Black bears, on the other hand, are subject to almost no restrictions (except a limit of three bears per year) or no closed season in most game management units. Shooting a sow with cubs is prohibited.

Probably, the most distinctive difference between a black bear and a grizzly/brown is the head, black bears' heads having a "straight" facial profile with a sharper snout that is a light tan/brown. Also the grizzly has a very noticeable shoulder hump, while the black bear has none. Both species have a wide variety of colors, ranging from white or blonde to coal black.

Bear meat should always be cooked well done. When cooked well done, it is perfectly safe but rare bear may carry the serious disease of trichinosis.

ARCTIC HUNTRESS' DAY

Amongst cottonwood's great golden puffs,
mixed with deep green spruce,
are scattered, brilliant, crimson strokes,
leaves of the currant bush.
Warm golden rays, fall on the rock,
frost vanishes as steam.
Frost sharpened blow, the scents of fall,
perfuming the faintest breeze.
She crouches there, beside me now.
With bated breath we watch.
Grey ghosts appear, in the morning mist,
from nowhere, as in a dream.
With widened eyes, and nostrils flared,
blood surging, hot in her veins,
she lifts her rifle, holds it tight.
It speaks, a crashing boom.
Mighty horns jerk up...and freeze;
then fall, and disappear.
She leaps, and runs, to the brush,
she parts it, and she sees.
She turns and calls, in a high sweet voice,
"A big one - and he's dead!"
I see her strut, coming back,
across the broken ground.
At camp that night, the meat was hung.
The stars stood crisp and bright.
Her hand crept snuggling, into mine,
in the still of night.
Ruddy campfire flickered, as we sat,
well content with the day, and our life.

AUTUMN WHIMSEY

Come hunting season, I always know that pretty soon, now, we are going to be getting those lovely, golden, fall days...frosty nights, crisp mornings and hot, sunny afternoons. Many days, though, we will have to watch out for those thick morning fogs.

I recall the time, here at my cabin on the Salcha...I got up at the first grey light of dawn, stumbled out the door... and discovered that I couldn't see a foot in front of my face. I couldn't see a hand in front of my face, either, I discovered, when I held my right hand up before my eyes. For obvious reasons, I didn't try to see two feet in front of my face — the fog was that thick.

Instead, I gave up in disgust, made sure both feet were on the ground, and went inside for another cup of coffee. Sometimes I'm a little goofy, first thing in the morning...If you don't believe me, ask Plum — she'll tell you!

It was just as well that I went back in — the thick fog made it impossible to see to shoot.

Speaking of shooting, I made the mistake of questioning Plum's shooting ability, back when we were first married. "Are you any good with that thing?" I challenged.

"You bet...I can hit a fly with this," Plum said, flourishing her rifle.

"I don't believe that for a minute," I scoffed.

With a quick motion, she jumped up and crushed a black fly against the window frame — with the butt of her rifle.

"There," she said, eyes mischievous, as she sat back down.

"Plum! That was really awful," I exclaimed, as I wiped the little crushed corpse and its ooze of goo off the wooden frame.

"Well, if you don't kill 'em, you are overrun with flies before you know it," she replied.

It was the pun that I considered awful. I never have been able to cure her of them, either... but you learn to live with it.

PART IV
FALL AND EARLY WINTER, THE HOLIDAYS

Winter is the time of year for fun in the snow. I hope you all have as much fun as we do.

IT LOOKS LIKE IT'S GOING TO BE A LONG WINTER (Fall 1992)

It has been a tough fall, no question about it. My boat is parked high on the gravel bar at my cabin, loaded down with hundreds of pounds of ice. But I feel fortunate that it is safe at home. More than a few are stranded for the winter on remote stretches of river and I sympathize with the worries of the owners.

Plum and I were hunting on the middle-fork of the Salcha river when we woke, the morning of September 16, to see the thermometer reading exactly zero... fahrenheit. This is not good when you are over 100 miles up river from the nearest road, in a boat. It was our first clue that it was time to put the boat away, the weather bureau had forecast sixty above for that day. But, then, that's why so many forecasters have to leave the state...the weather doesn't agree with them. Good thing the weather forecaster was not present. He would have suffered a severe tongue lashing, at the least. Since then, Plum has cooled off...a little.

There are a number of hazards to boating late in the season. I recall the time, mid-September again, that my nephew, Larry Curtis, and I came down river to the Salcha River landing. The ramp had a fine glaze on it from water dripping off boats and trailers. To make matters worse, unknown to us, the truck brakes were frozen.

Larry backed the trailer down the ramp, into the water, and touched the brakes. Nothing happened, and the truck continued slowly backward. Quick wittedly, he threw the truck into first. Good idea...but it didn't work. Wheels spinning on the glaze, the truck eased into the river.

Larry's eyes grew large and round, and his lips formed a rounded ooohhh! I had to laugh, even though it was my truck. Water flowed in the open window and rose over the hood, until only the ornament showed and my spluttering nephew emerged.

I have seen that happen one other time, to a friend named Cecil. As he marched out of the river, dripping, an incredulous tourist asked, "Now why did you do that?" Mixed expressions played across Cecil's face, while he obviously counted to ten before answering,

"Damn it, lady, I didn't do it on purpose!"

JUST A-FISHIN'
Larry wrung his hands and loudly moaned,
"I wish we hadn't slid right in, I wish we had a tow."
Just then I heard a motor boat, about to see our woe.
"Now Larry," I said, in urgent tone,
"Just hush up with your wishin'.
Take this rod in your hand...
and pretend we're just a-fishin'."

The end of summer always comes almost as a relief. During our short, golden season of warmth, we put in long days, seven days a week, working hard and playing hard to squeeze the most from summer, while it lasts.

Winter brings lengthening dusk and a more leisurely pace. It is a season for more time spent beside the fire or snow-machining out to visit friends. But winter has its hazards too.

Just yesterday, when I had relaxed for barely one well deserved month...just thirty days, Plum reminded me that one last chore remained to be done before I was ready for winter. I don't know why it is, but a woman just can't stand to see a man relax.

She wanted me to get the snow-machine running.

I grumbled and complained, but the woman was persistent. So I slipped on my bunny boots, hat, and coat and wandered out to my log shop building. There, in a dark corner of the parking deck, brooded a hulking, shadowy, sinister form...Hagar, The Horrible.

Hagar is, as you might have guessed, Swedish, a double track Ockelbo snow machine with a single ski. He had grown fat and lazy from a summer's rest, and resented being called upon for a new season of efforts.

Whistling, I sidled up to him casually, trying to pretend that this was a social call. He was not fooled...and continued to brood darkly, perhaps even threateningly.

Dry mouthed and sweaty handed, I fought a tremor of fear. I had to subdue it, for if a snow machine senses fear, it is all over. He will attack instantly.

I gathered my nerve and leaped boldly astride his seat, grasped the key, and turned it. The silence was deafening. Darn him, he had let his battery go dead, on purpose I'm sure.

I flipped on the enrichener and pumped the primer. Seizing the handle of the rewind rope, I gave it a mighty yank. That made him mad. With a loud snort he yanked back, nearly pulling my arms out of their sockets.

After a lengthy battle and lots of coughing and complaining, Hagar yielded to the inevitable. He let me mount, and ride him out across the snow.

The sly Swede had tricks still in reserve. Straight across the clearing he went, headed directly for the eight foot drop-off onto the frozen river. Frantically, I forced the handle bars into position for a hard right turn, throwing my full weight into the effort.

Hagar ignored my effort stubbornly and continued to roar across the snow toward the looming cliff. (These single ski machines don't turn well, in certain snow conditions) My heart thundered, my mouth was dry — now I was going to die!

With a last desperate cunning, I grabbed for his key, and shut it off before he noticed. Victory was mine. He was slowing. But it was too late. With his single ski turned sideways, Hagar hit a stump and rolled, slowly and majestically, all six hundred pounds coming to rest squarely atop my sprawled body.

Oh well, I thought, the black and blue marks should fade away in only a week or two — but it was not to be. More fun in the snow lay ahead...

When my sled passed me, I knew that I was in big trouble. It was my first clue, though I should have suspected I had a problem when my snow-machine started fishtailing on the glare ice.

From the corner of my eye, I noticed the sled disappear around the bend, just as my machine went into a high speed spin.

I didn't have a great deal of time to contemplate the problem, though, because I was busy hanging on — not well enough, and not for long.

They say that my screech, as I sailed off over the front of the machine (wiping off the windshield on the way) blighted all the willows in a hundred mile radius.

I don't believe that. I did notice all the brown, dying willows, last summer — but I think it is really mean of my friends to try to put me on a guilt trip over that. (Actually, I have discovered that it is an airborne blight that caused the willows to die).

Anyway, the windshield went with me, as I flew

off the machine and, when a sensitive part of my anatomy hit the unyielding ice I was sitting in the middle of the windshield. It wasn't broken (the windshield I mean — I'm not sure about my butt, it felt broken for some time) so I jumped up and flourished the windshield over my head triumphantly. I was showing off for Plum, who was rolling her eyes at me as she braked to a stop.

As always, when I show off, I ended up looking the fool. My feet shot out from under me on the glare ice and, this time, when I sat in the middle of the windshield, it shattered into a hundred fragments.

Troubles with snow machines and sleds are nothing new to me. We have had more trouble with self-destructing sleds than I could tell about, especially fold-a-sled types or anything with skis and suspensions. I'm sure it had nothing to do with us. Our standard operating procedure was to load up a sled with two hundred pounds. If it survived a round trip on the Salcha, we would put on four hundred pounds the next time. We were constantly cussing these flimsy sleds.

I don't believe that we ever had a sled that survived a third trip, until we got an akio type sled from Wit's Welding. I haven't been able to destroy it in six years, try as I might.

If any of you snow machine dealers have the courage to see if your brand will stand the test, I'll behappy to take one...free, of course. If it survives, I will give you a plug. If it doesn't, I'll give you my condolences. The line forms on the right.

Plum has a problem with sleds, too. Back in the days when we foolishly used to let her go in front, she knew only one position on the throttle — wide open. The sled banged over the bumps, strewing its mangled cargo piecemeal along the trail. Perish the thought of looking back. I muttered under my breath a lot. Stopping to pick up another of the scattered remains, crumpled, torn, smashed, I would stare at it bemusedly, wondering what in the world it used to be and why we were hauling it up river.

Finally, we would catch up with her where she was stuck, her empty sled upside down and wedged in between two spruce trees. Or sometimes, for variety, the sled would be upside down and stuck in a ditch. Nothing else ever made her stop.

Needless to say, we stopped letting her pull a sled.

Worst of all, though, is getting into overflow...and bogging down...and coming to a stop. As the machine settles beneath you, there is plenty of time to wonder how deep it is. Does the water go all the way to the bottom? How swift is the current? And, is it my day to die? That is a real "sinking" feeling, right in the pit of the stomach.

ARCTIC DAY

Stark black trunks of spruce loom
against all pervasive white.
Delicate, crystalline frost muffles the trees and brush.
Frost silences the world, soft at forty below.
Snowshoes break the silence with muffled crunch.
A form appears, bulky, parka bundled,
traveling, across the lonely land,
breath steaming from the hood.

She stops, parka hood swept back,
her hair ripples...a brilliant flame,
against the colorless land.
Restless emerald eyes scan for signs of life.
Across the whitened plain,
another rippling, brilliant flame springs forth,
twitching sharp nose lifted.
The fox scents the breeze - and freezes in alarm.

The rifle lifts, steadies.
Down the barrel, The emerald eyes gaze.
A puff of smoke. A muffled crack.
Crimson stains the snow.
Forty below steals warmth from the steaming blood.
Elated, she gathers the prize.

The muffled crunch of snowshoes fades toward the tiny cabin.
Silence settles on the land.
White snow, red stained,
tells a silent tale.
Stark black trunks of spruce loom
against all pervasive white.
Delicate, crystalline frost muffles the trees and brush.
Frost silences the world, soft at forty below.

(This poem won the $1,000 grand prize in the Spring 1992 Iliad Press Literary Awards Program.)

HALIBUT IN THE CHENA?

The other day, when I poked my head into the kitchen, Plum was busy whipping up a batch of cookies. I sniffed appreciatively. They smelled good. I glanced regretfully at the bulge above my belt.

"Oh, hi dear," she said, "Did you know that they are catching lots of halibut in the Chena?" (The Chena river flows through Fairbanks).

"Hmm!" I replied, "That is very interesting. Who is your source?"

"Ronnie Redfern," she said. "He told his mom and she told me."

Knowing Plum, I restrained my excitement, and called the source. He was working at his dad's shop -- Roger's Auto Repair.

Ronnie chuckled. "Well," he said, "between my mom and your wife they got it half right. But it's burbot we're catching, not halibut."

That sounded just as good. Burbot, known as 'poor man's lobster' is an excellent fish, either beer battered and deep-fried, or broiled and served with melted butter. With its bulbous head and snaky body, burbot is an ugly fish. Cheechakos, repelled by its ugliness, have been known to release it back into the river. What a mistake!

Burbot, sometimes called "fresh water lingcod",

is delicious by either name.

Ronnie has had excellent success spearing burbot in the Chena and good luck ice fishing season for burbot in the Tanana.

A favorite spot locally for burbot ice fishing sets is off the Chena Pump campground on the Tanana. But any place you can find a deep hole along the Tanana is a likely spot for a burbot set line, especially in back eddies by cliffs or at the confluence of a tributary. Ronnie's preferred bait is smelt (available at the grocery store).

When I called Fish and Game for regulations, I was given the following information, specifically for the Tanana and Chena rivers: The season is open year around for cither spearing or set lines, with a bag limit of fifteen per day. Set lines must have a total of no more than fifteen three quarter inch or less single hooks, whether it is one line with fifteen hooks or fifteen lines with one hook each. The weighted end of the line must rest on the river bottom.

Each set line must be tagged with the owner's name and address and must be checked at least once every twenty-four hours. This furnishes an ideal excuse to escape from the house for a pleasant outing, but don't let Plum know that I said so. Gotta go now, it's time to round up my ice fishing gear...Now let's see, where did I leave that ice augur?

WE GATHER TOGETHER

Last Thanksgiving day, my deep meditation was shattered...broken off in mid snore. My nose twitched. An alluring aroma called me, beckoning me up off my cozy living room chair, where I had been hard at work, and into the dining room.

The pies steamed on the table, mincemeat and pumpkin, my favorite. Whistling softly, I strolled across the room, nonchalantly, edging closer to the pies. My hunter's instincts were fully aroused. My nose twitched again. If I had a tail, it would have twitched, too.

I rolled my eyeballs furtively toward the kitchen. Good! I saw Plum bent over the oven, totally absorbed in basting the turkey. Silently, I slunk to the table, keeping a wary eye on her back.

There was no knife near the pies, I discovered. Ah well, luckily I had my Shrade Trapper's pocket knife handy. I dug it out and cut a small piece of the mince, hardly more than a quarter of the pie, which I popped in my mouth. I felt nervous and guilty...and it was fun, too.

The shriek, like a wounded eagle, pierced my guilty ears. I gasped, forgetting that inhaling sharply is not a good thing to do — not with a whole piece of pie in your mouth. I began to choke. I felt Plum beating on my back — and not, I suspected, because I was choking. The woman gets so emotional about petty pilfering. Fortunately, I got the pie down the right tube and fended off further blows.

"That pie is for company!" Plum informed me, emphatically, with a glare.

I hung my head, looking at her from under my brows. Sometimes, if I can look cute enough, that gets me off the hook. Not this time, though...she was really steamed.

A look of horror suddenly appeared on her face. "That's your skinning knife," she accused, "You've been skinning dead animals with it and then you used it to cut the pie."

"Naw," I soothed her, "I cleaned it after skinning." Her expression began to relax. "Besides," I added, "Gutting those fish yesterday would have taken off any musk that might have been left from the mink."

Silently, grim faced, she turned and crossed the room. I heard her sob, as she began to assemble another mince pie. You'd think she'd have learned to make me a pie all of my own...after all these years.

Anyway, it's that time of year that we gather together to eat turkey and stuffing and cranberry sauce and stuffed moose heart and butter beans and rolls and pickles and olives and mashed potatoes with gravy and, most of all, pie.

Oh, yeah, and to ask the Lord's blessing and give

thanks...I really didn't forget that.

We have so much to be thankful for, Plum and I: Each other, to start with (at least I'm thankful -- she may be prayerful, "Please, Lord, make him not be such a turkey."); Alaska, for another, and the Tanana valley and Salcha River...the grandeur, the room, the freedom and beauty. We've had a beautiful year to be thankful for — a warm, early spring, a long hot summer and a mild fall; and last, but not least, we're thankful for the two fine, big caribou bulls he sent to feed us through this winter.

Plum uses the following recipe for mince-meat pie — it's mighty tasty:

BETTY REDFERN'S MOOSE OR CARIBOU MINCE MEAT PIE

One unbaked 9" pie shell and upper crust
One 30 ounce jar of fruit mince meat mix
Enough diced or shredded cooked moose or caribou to fill the fruit mix jar (diced up left over roast works well)

Mix the fruit mix and shredded meat thoroughly, dump mixture into the pie shell and level, flop on top crust and seal by pinching around edges. Bake at 425 degrees for about 45 minutes or until nicely browned.

Easy as pie!

THE EXPERT WOODSMEN

My son, Mark came home for the holiday, on leave from his job on the tug boats at Valdez. As usual, we led each other astray.

This time, a birch tree near the cabin had accumulated too much snow. The big, old birch leaned heavily to the north, right toward the cabin. It worried me.

We talked it over.

The birch had to go, we decided. Busily, we began to assemble our tools...chain saw, we made sure the chain was sharp and tight and the fuel tank full...falling wedge, rope, come along...axe, just in case. We had a plan.

Plum came out and caught us at it. "What are you two up to?" she asked suspiciously.

We told her.

"Nooo!" she wailed, shaking her head back and forth violently, "leave it alone."

You would have thought she didn't trust our abilities. Women are so negative. I gently explained our strategy — and explained that the birch would fall on the cabin if we didn't cut it down.

Mark and I set to work felling the tree. We eyeballed it meticulously to determine the exact direction of the lean. We planned carefully, just how to fell it. We measured it, roped it and cranked it to one side with the come along. We sawed part way through the trunk and pounded in the wedge before finishing the cut...And we fell it right smack dab across the middle of the roof.

Mark vanished, like smoke, into the forest, before Plum even made it out the door...one second after the impact.

Boy! Was Plum proud of us, I mean really impressed. You should have heard her bragging on us to the neighbors. And, you know, it really wasn't that big a deal...about a hundred dollars worth of lumber and a week's work fixed that roof right up — almost as good as new.

THE BEST LAID PLANS

We eyeballed out the birch tree,
to see which way it leaned,
gathered up the chain saw,
sharp and tight and cleaned.
Out the window my wife watched.
I could see she was up tight.
But carefully we notched it,
so that birch would fall just right.
We cranked hard on the come-along,
to get the tree to lean.
We hammered in the wedge.
Man! We ain't so green.
They say careful planning pays off.
But I can't offer any proof.
You see, that darned old birch tree
lit square across the roof.

Not long after Thanksgiving, comes Christmas. Getting our own tree from the forest is one of our traditions.

OUR FIRST CHRISTMAS TREE

Many years ago, we prepared for our first Christmas at our cabin on the Salcha River. We started our preparations by setting out with a hatchet and sled to find our tree — the perfect tree.

My fingers stung in the thin monkey gloves. Somehow, too, loose snow had found its way down into my boot tops, to melt and saturate my pants legs. I fervently hoped that my ears, long since gone dead, hadn't broken off and got lost while I wasn't paying attention...I'd never find them in all this snow. Frost balled in my mustache and I wiped the annoying moisture under my numb nose with the back of my monkey glove.

It didn't matter — I was having fun...I knew because Plum told me so. Part of the joy of Christmas in the bush is spending hours searching through the snow and forest and out on the gravel bars through armpit deep snow, until you find the perfect tree.

Plum had already rejected quite a few.

We trudged out onto one more gravel bar. And there it stood, the perfect tree. Standing alone, it was

full and relatively symmetrical, not like so many
smaller trees that are grossly deformed by
crowding.

"Look at this one, Plum," I shouted; "Let's take
it."

She eyed it dubiously.

Well, so ok, it was maybe a little lopsided. I mean,
you know how Alaskan spruce get. And the branches
might be spaced a little oddly, with a gap here and
there — but I remembered my Dad fixing that sort
of problem with a drill and extra branches. And
maybe it was a little wider, in places, than it was
tall. Actually, on reflection, I must admit it maybe
even looked ugly, in a cute sort of way — but not
bad, for an Alaskan Spruce. Besides, it was here,
now, not on some other bar on up the river. It was
the perfect tree. I wanted it!! Visions of a roaring
barrel stove and a steaming mug of hot chocolate
obsessed me.

"I can't really see the tree's shape with all that
snow on it," Plum complained.

Without thinking too hard about it, I grabbed the
trunk and gave it a good shake to clear the snow.
Unfortunately, in order to grab the trunk I had to
stand under the tree. Next thing I knew the world
went white...I fell, crushed to my knees, gasping for
breath — then bounded erect with a shriek, as my
collar funneled icy crystals down my neck and into
my inner sanctum. The thrill of the chill is hard to

describe to anyone who hasn't experienced it.

My shrieks subsided as Plum consoled me, patting my back to make the snow melt faster, and saying, "Ok, we'll take it."

But the struggle was not over, I discovered, as the dull hatchet bounced off the frozen trunk. The tree, it seemed, rejected the honor we planned for it. Rage and brute force prevailed. I finally beat off enough frozen chips to be able to wrench the little spruce from its trunk.

Later, warmed by the fire and mugs of chocolate, we admired the Christmas tree and I admitted that it is part of the joy of a bush Christmas...getting your own tree.

(Incidentally, back in those newly wed days, I called the wife both Tootsie-roll and Sugar-plum. She says that she is mighty glad that, when I settled on one nickname it was Plum instead of Roll).

A CHRISTMAS PLEA

Cookies, candy, things like that,
    all contribute to my fat.
It doesn't seem quite fair, to me,
that that's the way things should be.

Everything that's good to taste
ends up growing 'round my waist.
    Furthermore, truth to tell,
I gain weight just from the smell.

Merry Christmas, the greeting sounds.
    I just gained ten more pounds.
    Santa, please, under the tree,
leave some will power just for me.

A SALCHA RIVER CHRISTMAS

In late October things slow down here in Alaska's interior. It's time to throw another log on the fire, relax, and admire the fluffy snow drifting by the windows.

"Oh yes," Plum says, "you do that so well — relaxing, I mean."

That's what I call my wife — Plum. She has crept up on me and is reading over my shoulder again. It's a bad habit of hers.

Just after Thanksgiving, when I had relaxed for, well, only about six weeks, Plum was at me again. I don't understand why that woman just can't stand to see a man relax. Now, she wanted me to take her to town...Christmas shopping for the relatives, all those foreigners down in the deep south. (To me, the deep south is anything south of the north city limits of Anchorage, Alaska).

Going to town shopping, you have to understand, is a major expedition. The river, of course, had places where it had not yet frozen thick enough to be sure of safety in running snow machines down it. So we had to go up over the hills. Thirty-five miles you have to bang your butt across country on a snow machine. 'Life threatening' is the only way to describe the experience. Horrifying drops loom at every bend of the trail, straight down. Just to contemplate the trip makes my hair stand on end, or it would if I had hair. The only consolation is that if you miss a turn the fall won't hurt you — the bottom is so far down that you would starve to death before splattering on the rocks. Terrific!

Then you get to the highway. Ahead lies another fifty miles to town on a slippery road, clutching the steering wheel with sweaty, white knuckled hands.

And the crowds?...Last time we went in, we barely got to the highway, and there were three people — I mean all in a group! It's enough to give a bush dweller cold chills.

Plum insisted on heading off to town, over my violent objections. I will spare you the details of the beating, no the maiming, I took — no, not from Plum... though I'm sure she would do it if necessary... but from my snow machine, Hagar, as we pounded off down the trail toward that northern metropolis, Fairbanks.

The Christmas lights and decorations of North Pole and Fairbanks were heartening — cheerful and bright. Against my will, I felt the glow of Christmas spirit suffusing me. I even burst into a very fine bass rendition of "White Christmas," until Plum's look of pain brought me to a stop.

"Please don't sing," she whispered urgently.

The woman doesn't even appreciate a fine male voice. Why, I'll have you know, I even used to sing in the church choir.

Suddenly, I found myself confronted by a freeway. One like the freeways that are part of my reason for staying away from Los Angeles, Seattle and such places. Here I thought that I knew every inch of Fairbanks. But they had been up to something while I was gone.

I found myself sucked into a mad whirl of traffic, ingested by the freeway. It rushed me off into unknown dimensions, through the dark. Nervously, I waited for the theme of "Twilight Zone" to begin to play.

Just as I began to despair, feeling that I was caught forever in a time-warp, the freeway spit me out. I was on a dark and lonely road amidst an eerie winter forest. After an hour of aimless driving, Plum made me stop at a house amongst the trees and ask directions — this, despite my loud denials that I was lost.

I preserved some tatters of Christmas spirit and even went off by myself next morning to do some shopping for Plum.

The first place I walked into had rows of vending machines, whirring, clanking, flashing lights... practicing all sorts of deceptions to lure a man into parting with his money. For a moment, I thought that I had been transported to Las Vegas.

One machine caught my eye, it promised coffee. That sounded good to me. I have a hard time doing anything until I get my morning dose of caffeine.

I advanced toward the machine, nervously. Now don't get me wrong. I've got guts. Give me a grizzly bear to grin down or wrestle and I'm perfectly at home. It's just that these machines are a little more intimidating than a grizz.

Anyway, I got out my four quarters. Gingerly, I fed them to the machine, and jumped back.

The red lights flashed, the machine rumbled and gave out a sort of muted si-reen sound. As I watched in surprise, that clever machine poured coffee with cream out of a spout atop a little square opening. And then, to my amazement, that machine drank the coffee straight down through a drain grate at the bottom of the opening. If I had had a cup, and was faster than I am, I could have caught me a cupful.

Now that's what I call real progress, eliminating the middle man. A machine that takes your money, brews you a cup of coffee, and then drinks it itself — just to save you the trouble.

Whooooeee!! What won't they think of next?

The experience did nothing to satisfy my craving for a good cup of coffee. Actually, it made me a little grumpy, as I reflected on it. About that time, a man opened up the machine, filled the coffee, sugar and cream containers, and filled an empty tube with cups.

So I got a cup of coffee. It was not good coffee. It tasted sort of like it had been brewed from water wrung out of my socks after I had been wading in the swamps of the Tanana Flats. But how I got to know that taste is another story, a long story.

At least I got my caffeine fix.

Well, being early, I got my shopping for Plum finished before the crowds began to thicken. Good thing, for soon I found myself pushing, shoving... snarling urban Christmas spirit with the best of them. Shopping does not bring out the best in us.

Somehow we survived the crowds, the roaring swarms of traffic, the ice fog, and the trip back to the blessed peace of the cabin. Don't ask me how. I struggled through it all in a daze, sort of like shock. Instinctively protecting my sanity, I guess.

The rest of the Christmas season was a joy. We found a spruce tree we liked out on the gravel bar, cut it down, and dragged it into the cabin. We soon had it decorated with freshly strung garlands of popcorn and Lifesavers, and frosted Christmas cookies, strung on thread.

Ah yes, the cookies. Unfortunately, more ended up in my belly than on the tree. This is a tough time of year for calorie-challenged middle aged men. Seems like Plum always shrinks my pants in December.

Christmas is a very social week on the Salcha with merry neighbors visiting back and forth on snowmachines. One year one of our neighbors had a cookie exchange party. Each couple brought a dozen plates of cookies they had baked to exchange for a plate of cookies from each of the others.

Not many cookies were eaten at the party, but the contents of a huge bucket of punch vanished. All the guests were full of Christmas spirits when they left. One, fuller of spirits than the others, arrived home with no cookies. The first traveler next day saw why, a trail of brightly wrapped plates of cookies led down the river to the reveler's door step.

We do know how to have fun on the Salcha river, and a very merry Christmas is had by all.

AN ARCTIC CHRISTMAS

Orange flickers of light
brighten our ruddy faces.
An orange look of warmth
is cast into the room.
As we stoke our barrel stove,
frost steams from our clothes.
In my mustache, balls of ice melt and drip.
Frosty fingers sting with returning blood.
Cheeks burn, toes tingle.

The tea kettle's whistle speaks comfortingly
of steaming mugs.
Hot chocolate, gratefully swallowed,
what bliss!
Outside, Northern Lights dance, ghostly green,
great crackling banners
streaming across the star lit sky.
Stark, black, spruce embrace our cabin home.

A pot of stew bubbles,
sending forth its savory scent.
Orange flickering light,
from the stove's open door,
lights the room.
Orange light dances and shines,
reflected from our tree,
decorated with tinsel, glass bulbs, cookies -
and popcorn we strung with happy laughter.

Twined in each other's arms,
we join in silent thanks
for the peace of our Arctic solitude.
Orange flickers warm our hearts,
on Christmas Eve.

'TIS THE SEASON

A walk through our woods at Christmas time is like a stroll through a fairyland. The fresh, sparkling snow on the ground and the patterns of frost in the spruce and birch are like priceless works of art — a study in black and white...against the golden haze of the rising/setting sun, low on the southern horizon.

I find myself creeping silently through the stillness of the forest, calmed by the peace. Here and there, a rose hip or high bush cranberry hangs on the underbrush, lending a bright spot of red or orange to the scene.

Everywhere there are stories to be read in the snow...here, the tiny trail of a shrew, running from one den to another, there the hop hop marks of the rabbit. Scattered remnants of cone mark the spot where a squirrel has dined on seeds from the spruce cones. Large tracks, accompanied by the prints of tiny hooves, show that a cow moose and her calf have moved out of the thicket, just ahead of me, to judge by the crisp edges of the prints...if I'm quiet, perhaps I can see them. I moved on, with a sense of expectancy.

In another spot, I came across mute evidence of a tragedy, written in the snow — a red spot of blood, a scattering of grey feathers, fox tracks leading to and from the spot and a trampled area in the snow where the fox had enjoyed a grouse for dinner.

"Life ends for some," I thought, "in order that it can go on for others."

I turned back toward the cabin, walking beneath black arches of spruce, white trimmed. It seemed like a temple.

Two grouse hung at my belt...plenty of dinner for Plum and me. As I neared the cabin, the sharp tang of burning spruce perfumed the air. A string of bright colored lights winked gaily from the cabin eves.

I stomped into the cabin, knocking the snow from my boots and closing the door firmly behind me. Returning blood, drawn by the warmth, stung my fingers and cheeks. And she greeted me with a kiss and a cup of warm cocoa. The odor of baking cookies scented the air with ginger and molasses.

Crackling flames in the barrel stove beckoned us into the living room, where we sat, sipping cocoa and admiring our Christmas tree.

Life doesn't get much better than this.

THE BARE AFFAIR

Ooops...that should have read the bear affair. Oh well, it caught your eye, didn't it?...and shame on you!

At times following, an exceptionally short summer or early winter, the bears haven't gotten enough food. Then, the grizzly bears on the Salcha River defy tradition and refuse to go to sleep for the winter. Instead, they stay up to raid cabins for goodies. Their breaking and entering is quite messy.

It sometimes seems that everything you meet out here is hungry: the wolves, the mosquitos, the old sourdoughs, the bears...They have been known to charge a camp, drawn in by the smell of frying bacon. Yep, some old sourdoughs are pretty rough customers when they're hungry. Several months alone in the wilds seems to draw out the worst in us. But no one will get hurt, so long as they don't stand directly between the charging sourdough and the frying pan...that's a good way to get trampled.

But the mosquitos are hungriest. Oh yes, especially the mosquitos. They should be our national bird. Certainly, they are big enough and numerous enough to defeat any other claimant for the title. The mosquitos just suck them dry leaving only a dried up bundle of feathers. I swat them myself, the mosquitos, that is, not the birds. I know, that is a sensitive thing to confess in these politically correct days. I hear that some weird ones in the Lower Forty-Eight plan to boycott Alaskan tourism, unless we cease all attempts at mosquito control, including swatting. That is just fine with me. I think I'll keep on swatting, thank you.

Getting back to bears, though. We share our country with a good many of them. I remain always aware of that fact when enjoying The Great Land. Through a number of incidents, I have formed some conclusions about bears.

Bears have peculiar appetites. Their preference appears to run to rubber products (sorry, I can't tell you why) favoring most highly the rubber seats of snow machines and A.T.V.s...like four wheelers, closely followed by radiator hoses and oil lines, though they enjoy a chew of tasty four wheeler tire, at times. Motor oil is a highly desirable beverage, with liquid soap close behind.

Fortunately for our noses, rotten salmon — after the spawning run— is high on the bear's list of favorite food. They perform a real service cleaning up this garbage.

When the bears can't get rubber products, motor

oil, rotten salmon or other garbage, they come after what we humans consider food.

Then is when we are in trouble.

Bears are curious creatures and will bite anything. Several times, I have chuckled, as I looked at the bite marks in a previously pressurized can of mosquito spray, visualizing the look on the bear's face when he bit into that can. I wish that I could see that, just once, from a safe distance.

In the forest, a person needs to keep constantly aware of the possible presence of bears. They can show up unexpectedly, just when you least expect them.

I recall the night that a friend was awakened from a sound sleep, in his hunting cabin, by a scratching at the door. Sleepily, he got up to open the door and let Red Dog come in. Just as he touched the door knob, some instinct of self preservation (or maybe it was an angel) reminded him that he had not brought Red Dog on this trip. Um-hmm, it was a bear. It left, without trouble. But, next morning, a nauseous pile on the doorstep confirmed the identity of the nighttime caller.

Another friend, wanting to keep his weekend cabin free of tantalizing odors, made a habit of dumping his bacon grease and cooking oils down the

outhouse hole. One day, his daughter sat down com-
fortably on the padded seat and began to tinkle. An
ominous snarl brought her up off the seat. As she
went out the outhouse door, she glanced back, to
see the head of a large grizzly come up through the
hole -- wet on top. Needless to say, they now burn
their grease, thoroughly.

Enough of this. If you can figure out the moral of
this story, please let me know. I think I'll mosey on
out with the twenty-two and see if I can catch some·
rabbits for supper.

BEAR BELLS

We were sitting 'round the camp,
relaxed and unaware,
soaking in the peace and calm,
from the country air.

Across the creek, we saw a bear
rear up and stand erect.
But we were still without a care,
our bear bells close to hand.

I shook the bells, a ringing sound -
carried clearly to the bear.
Growling, snarling, he turned around.
We began to feel a scare.

He came our way, we were all unnerved.
To him those bells meant dinner was served.
Stealthy like a cat he crept,
gliding through the brush.

We backed away from the camp.
We huddled in a bunch.
Fearfully, we watched the bear,
gobble up our lunch.

You may have heard bears mean no harm,
that they are cute creatures full of charm.
They harbor no malice, it is true;
only when hungry, will they eat you.

PART V DEEP WINTER

In January, February...March, winter stalks the land, with temperatures of fifty below, ice fog, a stifling blanket of white on the land - and, in the sky, blackness, twenty hours a day, relieved only by brief hours of grey twilight.

MINUS SIXTY

Clumsy hands and stinging face,
it seems I walk on knives.
I still feel, by heaven's grace.
Pain's end means only death.
Stiff fingers, feeling warm and nice,
won't bend the way they should.
Put in my mouth, they feel like ice.
To my teeth, they are hard as wood.
Desperate tears sting my eyes
and freeze my lashes tight.
Rubbing helps, but not a lot.
I've begun to lose my sight.
Stumbling blind, I must keep on.
I fall and rise again,
and stumble toward the Arctic dawn,
stark black, and white, and grey.
And then I fall and can't get up.
The snow seems soft and fine.
I cannot bend my arms or legs.
Black ravens line up to dine.
Somehow it doesn't matter now,
my white bed is soft and warm.
It folds me in a soft embrace;
I'll just close my eyes a while.

Not all is grim in these months. New Year's Eve has its festivities, of course, and snowmachining continues...during the warmer spells.

NEW YEAR'S IRRESOLUTION

New year's day...a time for resolutions. I never need to worry about thinking up any. Plum makes mine for me: things like losing weight, working harder, spending less time lounging on the deck and rambling through the woods.

Funny, though, the resolutions never seem to work. A month goes by, then two, and I'm as portly as ever...and I can't seem to muster much enthusiasm for work, particularly if I can come up with a good excuse to be off rambling through the forest and along the crick. But the resolutions make her happy, for a while.

But then, I'd guess that New Year's resolutions usually don't work. Most often having been made too light heartedly, without serious enough thought as to the consequences.

Losing weight, for instance. Sure, it's easy to say, "Yeah! I resolve to lose thirty pounds." But think about what that really means — not eating...at all. Well, maybe a couple lettuce leaves — with no dressing. And maybe a small piece of recycled cardboard, passing itself off as a diet cracker — and sold for four times the price of something good. No fat, for sure, and that's what I miss the most. Even cold CRISCO, straight from the can, begins to sound good.

Perhaps the worst part of these unrealistic resolutions is that they make me feel like a loser, a weakling. Come February 14, I have not only not lost the thirty pounds (in spite of grevious suffering) but that lying scales says that I've gained a couple pounds. I wonder if Plum could be messing with the scales. Depression sets in...and what better cure for depression than some chocolate candy! And there it is. My sweetie has gotten me a box, just for this day, but only a small one, since I'm dieting — what sadism, rubbing a man's nose in his own weak inadequacy. I snap, shoveling chocolate into my mouth with both hands, until it's all gone. Yep, you guessed it...next day I've gained another five pounds...from a one pound box of chocolates. Now, how could that happen? But it does.

This year I boldly decided that I'd make my own resolutions, ones that I can keep, that make me feel like a winner. Like, for instance, a resolution to not gain any weight. That's tough enough, but do-able. Or, for instance, working harder, at prospecting and writing, though Plum, I fear, would consider that to be spending more time lounging on the deck and rambling through the woods. Ah well, at least I would know I had succeeded.

I informed Plum of this plan and she was not happy. But I stuck to my guns and she finally agreed. Speaking of sticking to your guns, I grabbed mine bare handed the other day after it had been sitting outdoors — what a mistake. Remember Robert Service's line?..."A careless feel of a bit of steel burns like a red hot coal."

I'll let you know how it works out. Maybe we can start a whole new trend in New Year's resolutions.

'SNO FUN

The Fairbanks and North Pole area offers hundreds of miles of individual snowmobile riding possibilities and also organized activities such as racing. There are cross country races, oval races and drag races (no that doesn't mean burly, bearded men racing while dressed in sun dresses and flowered bonnets).

I learned something about snowmachining, one day a number of years ago, while roaring across a shoulder of the Alaska Range in a mist of flying powdered snow, beneath the brilliant blue Alaskan skies and golden winter sun. Ah, the exhilaration of fresh air, speed, motion.

Plum and I stopped on the mountain's edge, looking out over Fielding Lake, far below. Our group of friends caught up to us and stopped, too.

Our saddle bags held enough ptarmigan for a tasty dinner and, though we didn't know it yet, our set lines in the lake held burbot — "poor man's lobster". What a way to live.

Looking back, we could see the long, winding, gently climbing route we had taken to this point. It would take quite awhile to go back down that way and our bellies rumbled with hunger.

A dozen year's ago, or so, when this took place, I

was still young enough to be foolishly over-confident. "Watch me," I shouted, "I'll show you how it's done." The hill didn't look bad...a little steep but fairly smooth...this would be simple, a piece of cake. Straight down the slope I went, faster and faster. My guts churned with that same sensation I feel on rollercoasters with names like "Suicide Drop" or "Sudden Death." A sudden feeling possessed me, a feeling that I had made a terrible mistake, but I had no options, just hang on and pray.

About midway down, a sharp swell ran diagnolly across the ridge, forcing my skis to the left before it disappeared. After a brief floating feeling, as I soared through the air, the ground came up and slapped me hard. I continued to roll down the hill — unfortunately, with the snow machine rolling sideways behind me, catching up every few feet to beat me with its handle bars and skis, until it finally leaped over me and continued down the hill.

At the bottom of the ridge, my machine ended up right side up on the lake, still running and ready to ride, unhurt except a missing windshield. I dragged my aching body astride it and collapsed to rest. Then I noticed that they had all abandoned me, heading back around the long way down — even though I'd shown them how it was done. Even Plum had abandoned me — can you imagine that?

By pure luck, nothing was broken, although my body was one giant black and blue bruise for weeks.

The experience could have killed me.

New riders, be careful.

Generally speaking, early season lake ice is thinner in the center than along the shoreline traveling at high speed can generate a wave effect that will shatter the ice ahead of your snowmobile. Test the ice before being the first to run a new route.

Some rivers here don't freeze real well until on into December or January. In places, warm springs (34 degrees or so is warm in the midst of an Alaskan winter) keep the ice thin all winter, often with water over the top of it -- the whole covered by a treacherously deceptive blanket of snow. It looks good until you are in the middle of it -- bogged down. Then, as the machine settles beneath you, there is plenty of time to wonder how deep it is...is there another layer of ice, or does the water go all the way to the bottom?

Bruising or breaking your body...or drowning...'sno fun.

Along that line of thought, FEAR OF HEIGHTS plagues some of us, including Plum. Some years ago, five or six, I believe, Plum and I made a winter caribou hunting trip down near Healy...over across the Nenana River in the Boot Hill area. Rumor had it that a big herd of caribou had concentrated there. Since light snow blanketed the ground, a group of us headed south with our snow machines to get ourselves some meat.

We had instructions on how to reach the railroad bridge across the Nenana River...And we found it all right.

Plum, for once, was speechless. We stared into the depths of the yawning chasm...down at the foaming white water, far below. A walkway, about three feet wide ran along one side of the bridge for snow machine access.

It took a great deal of gathering up her courage for Plum to edge her machine slowly and gingerly across to the far bank. Her face, when she arrived, was whiter than the snow. And she confides that she didn't enjoy the day at all, for she was tormented by thoughts of the return trip across that bridge.

That evening, we returned to our vehicles. And just guess who got caught in the middle of the bridge when the freight train roared by — 18 inches away? Yup...Plum, clutching the guard cable, with her eyes tight closed, quivering in terror. We haven't made that trip again.

YUKON QUEST

Black velvet, the backdrop of Arctic night,
pierced by points of twinkling white.
Gauzy, glimmering, ghostly, green
rippling curtains waver 'cross the scene
And across the pole star,
home of the dead,
wavers a curtain of shimmering red.
Now, from the hush of the Arctic night,
grows a sibilant hiss from out of sight.
Whistling sled runners?...
the ghost team's breath!
racing 'cross the sky, undeterred by death.

In January, sled dog racing season is nearly upon us. First is the Alpirod, run in Europe during January. Many Alaskan mushers participate.

Then, the Yukon Quest, in February, tests the skill and stamina of the mushers and teams on a 1,000 mile wilderness course that runs between Fairbanks and Whitehorse (the starting point alternating between Fairbanks and Whitehorse, year to year). Many a story is told by Yukon Quest contestants of ghostly companions who accompany them a ways along the trail...the spirits of teams and mushers who have gone before. And who knows? Alone, out there in the cold blackness, with the Northern Lights running wild...you, too, might become a believer in the ghost team.

Next, the world championship sled dog race coincides with the mid-February, Anchorage Fur Rendezvous and consists of three 25 mile heats on three consecutive days. Considerable numbers of festive events are scheduled for Rendezvous week and a good time is had by all.

March brings the Iditarod Trail Sled Dog Race, another 1,000 mile race...running from Anchorage to Nome, along the traditional dog sled mail route. This is the trail taken by the mushers who made the famous 1925 run to Nome with serum to stop the diphtheria epidemic.

Last, but far from least, is the Open North American Sled Dog Championship, held in Fairbanks in late March. This race consists of two twenty-mile heats and, on the third day, a thirty mile heat.

These races are a tribute to our northern history and a celebration of our Alaskan tradition and culture. Even for non-mushers, these events provide touches of excitement, color and festivity during what would otherwise be a rather dreary season.

We have always had a special relationship, we Alaskans, with Hawaii — often fleeing there for a recharge, a relief from winter's stresses. These next two poems are about the islands.

ARCTIC INTERLUDE

It was minus forty when we left,
our home white shrouded in snow.
Long hours of dark had left their mark,
our spirits were drooping low.

We climbed aboard the jumbo jet,
soared into the icy sky.
As we flew on south through the night,
the moon rose full and high.

We came down through the velvet night
and landed near Waikiki.
Soft tropic moon cast golden light
in a path across the sea.

Silhouetted against the moon,
trembling in warm, perfumed breeze,
the palm trees' fronds whispered soft,
of a life of tropic ease.

Though we love our Arctic home,
cold and dark sometimes make us flee
to tropic palms and tropic sands
and breakers of a tropic sea.

TROPIC DAWN

Stretching far to either side,
in tropic pre-dawn grey,
foaming surf outlined in white
the curving beach, Ki-hei.
I stepped into the surging warmth,
it broke with a hollow boom.

Black against the morning grey,
I saw Ka-hoo-la-we loom.
Against the slowly greying sky,
the horizon was stark and black.
Sparkling night lights on the coast,
from the water, reflected back.

I turned to face toward Maui now,
warm surf surged round my knees.
Lovely, exotic, tropic palms,
whispered in the breeze —
every fiber of every frond
silhouetted clear and stark.

A wash of pink grew across the sky,
to slowly banish dark.
Ha-le-ak-ala wore a rosy crown,
pink puffs of cloud were west.
Amongst a spreading golden glow,
the sun rose from its rest.

At other times, we escape winter's grip to the mecca of Nevada. It's always fun and, sometimes, we get a little slap-happy...as you can tell by this story.

HIGH TIMES

They are getting mighty proud of their drinks on the airlines. Four dollars each, they get for them now. I'm just a hick from the Alaskan bush and don't get to travel much. Once, perhaps, every five years, or so, I travel south for the bright lights and some hot casino action. Imagine my shock, when I discovered the disheartening run up in drink prices during a recent flight to Las Vegas...Last time I flew, the drinks were only one dollar each.

Why, for the price of two drinks, I could buy a whole bottle of the good stuff and bring my own drinks...carefully concealed, of course, in a brown paper bag. I could lean back, leading the life of ease, sip surreptitiously from the bag, from time to time, and no one would be the wiser.

If a young lady down the aisle caught my eye, I could gallantly offer her a shot at my bag. Wouldn't that impress her? Maybe I could even start a new fad.

Certainly, it would lend a whole new meaning to the term "brown bagging". This sounds like just the sort of thing the Yuppies would eat up...Cheap, environmentally sensitive - instead of all those little throw-away bottles and cups, just one big bottle and a reusable brown bag.

It could even develop into a major social event — bag parties on the airline. Getting there really would be half the fun. Come to think of it, getting there might be all the fun, since many of us wouldn't remember much about what happened after we landed.

I can see it now, as we stagger down the aisle, holding each other up, on our way to get off the plane, the stewardess looks at the pilot and says, "I just don't understand it...no one bought anything to drink on this flight."

Despite the hazards of travel, we did survive the:

LAS VEGAS ODYSSEY

Sin city...Las Vegas! Plum and I had arrived. We had come in search of sun...and fun. Nothing that we had heard about Vegas had prepared us for what we were about to experience.

The dull roar of conversation, punctuated by whoops and cheers while coins hammered into the payoff tray, was accompanied by the chirps, beeps and chimes of slot machines. A full rendition of the Hallelujah Chorus rose above the din — someone had hit the big one. Lights flashed and whirled everywhere across the room, gold, red, yellow and vibrant green, whirling and   beckoning. My blood pressure rose. The pulse hammered in my ears. Veins stood out at   my temple and my right arm began to twitch convulsively.

I ducked behind a nearby bank of slot machines, took my wallet out of my pocket and craftily stuffed it in my boot top. Sweat misted my forehead, while I glanced around to make certain that I was unobserved. After all, we were in the big city.

We got one hundred dollars worth of quarters and set off across the endless room, dropping in coins, pulling levers, and pushing buttons.

That first hundred dollars vanished like smoke. I looked at my watch. We had been in Vegas half an hour, and already we were down a hundred. But we had won our way through to the baggage claim area. After seeing the airport, I could hardly wait to experience a real casino.

I tried to pull Plum away from the change machine she was playing. "But I'm winning, " she protested. She put in another dollar. Four quarters came out. "See," she said. With a pitying look, I assured her that the hotel would have machines just like this one, and pried her fingers loose. Big mistake...I later discovered that these were the best odds in town.

An official looking, uniformed person was standing nearby. We showed him our tickets and asked, "Where will our bags be coming off?"

He replied, "Ten to one says they will come off on console number three." He looked serious! I should have taken the bet, though, because they came off on number seven. I could have made a mint.

In due course, we arrived at our 'hotel'. It looked like a circus tent huddled between King Arthur's castle and a Star Wars space vessel. As we walked in the door, a running wookie nearly knocked us over. He cried, "Stampede!" and we ducked behind a flying buttress long enough to let the seven frightened elephants thunder by, pursued by an armored knight and a Darth Vader look alike. What a mess. A colossal pooper scooper was urgently needed. No, I wasn't that frightened — the elephants were apparently not house broken. The crowd at the lunch show was mightily disappointed at the escape of the entertainment.

Daunted, we gazed off across the vast distances. There must be some sort of space warp inside this building. (I later learned that there were 4,500 rooms and ten eating places in this one hotel. The casino was scaled to match.) Maid Marian and a Klingon warlord were engaged in conversation nearby.

"Pardon me," I said to Maid Marian, with a timid glance at the Klingon, "Can you tell me where the registration desk is?"

She pointed through the maze of machines, and said "That way — two furlongs."

I gasped in dismay.

"Beware," she said softly, "Therein lurk more treacherous traps, manned by live dealers."

Resigned, I got two hundred dollars worth of change, hoping it would be enough to win through to the registration desk. It was — barely. After creeping by the monstrous tank of live sharks, we registered. That must be where people go who exceed their gambling budget and can't pay...shark food.

Aside from gambling, I discovered that everything in Vegas is cheap. The drinks are free, under the theory (evidently) that all the free booze you can drink while playing will loosen your attachment for that green stuff, in the wallet you have stuffed in your boot. (Yep, that's what all us hicks do with it). A prime rib dinner can be had for as little as three ninety-five. First class rooms are available for twenty-nine dollars a night, sometimes less. Both a trolley ($1.00) and city buses ($1.25) run the length of the strip. Casino hopping is fascinating, especially at night, amidst the glitter and flash of all the lights, punctuated by eruptions of the spectacular volcano in front of the Mirage casino.

During our trip, we drove down into Arizona for a couple days, to Lake Havasu on the Colorado River.

It is a different, but pleasing country, offering out-door opportunities. We saw a number of boats fish-ing on the quiet water and wished we had planned a longer stay in Arizona. From Las Vegas reasonably priced rafting trips on the Colorado river are avail-able, as are air or ground excursions to the Grand Canyon.

Plum and I enjoyed our trip. Best of all, I even came back north with a touch of tan. Sixty in the shade translates into reasonable weather for tanning by the pool, for us Alaskans. It made a nice break from our long winter and, now, I might even make it to spring.

I wish that I could boast of coming back with some money. Some do, I have heard, though I'm not sure how credible a rumor that is. But, then, you can't have everything. I will say, though, that I was mighty glad to get that wallet out of my boot when we headed north...it was wearing a terrible blister on my ankle.

Eventually, winter passes, making way for another golden Alaskan spring. A sense of the grand cycle helps us endure the bitterest, weeks.

'NEATH THE MIDNIGHT SUN

Circling 'round the azure dome,
of the northern sky,
never sleeping midnight sun,
lights our arctic home.
Three months long, the golden day,
for a year of work and fun.

Midnight's golden glow oft finds
us still at work or play.
We sleep less now, not to waste,
summer's one long golden day.
Death of summer soon will bring,
autumn's frosty taste.

Summer's one long golden day,
'neath the midnight sun,
fades away to velvet night
and the mid-day moon.
Crackling, wavering, greenish light,
Aurora is at play.

Fifty below, blowing snow,
winter rules the land.
Crisp and cold, approaching spring,
every day at noon,
with brief, grey hours of dim light,
promises rebirth.

PART VI
MORE ALASKAN TALES

OF HATS AND DOGS...AND EVEN WIVES

Men treasure their hats. They really do. My boating hat, for instance, has become an old friend. It has been with me through boat wreck and storms, fishing trips, prospecting and hunting. Properly seasoned with fish slime and caribou blood, molded to my head by the rain, its crown broken down to a comfortable slouch, it's a perfect hat. Through many a successful hunt, it has become my lucky hat and hunting without it would be unthinkable, tempting the fates.

And Plum hates it!

It's odd how, just when a man gets his hat properly broken in, his woman develops a hate for it. Inevitably, she wants to wash it — thereby destroying the bill, which takes on a wavy configuration that makes its wearer look like a certified doofus. Laundering a hat also washes away the magic.

The hat before this one, about eight years ago, had reached the same state of perfection. Plum constantly eyed it with disgust. "Let me get rid of it," she pleaded, "I'll buy you a new one.''...like consoling someone whose dog has died with, "I'll buy you a new one.''...as though they were mass produced, interchangeable units...ignoring the emotion invested in the relationship, the years it takes to develop a treasured relationship with a dog...or a hat — or even a wife.

One day, in her bookkeeping office, she spotted a well treasured hat lying unguarded on a chair. "Here's my chance," she thought, "Ted will never know what happened to it." With a slinking feline ...oops, I mean feminine...motion, she pounced, seized the hat, dropped it into the garbage and emptied the coffee grounds on it. Smugly she sat back at her desk, to work on some bookkeeping that Melvin Quakenbush had just dropped off.

Next morning, Melvin came back through the door. "Dottie," he said, "I've lost my hat — I think I left it here. Have you seen it?"

Blushing with well deserved chagrin, Plum said, "Was that your hat?...About that hat, Melvin...I thought it was Ted's and threw the rotten old thing away. The garbage man already picked it up."

Melvin said no more about it but, to this day, Melvin keeps a firm clutch on his hat when he visits us.

PUTTING THE OUTHOUSE IN PLUMBIN', MECHANICIN' AND OTHER MISDEMEANORS

Every so often, my wife Plum comes up with a new project for me to do around our cabin, here on the mid-reaches of the Salcha River.

Recently, Plum made me put the toilet in. I fought it for years, mostly because I hate doing plumbing (not to mention the fact that I'm just naturally opposed to work, on principle). Think of all the technological improvements that have been made...computers, airplanes, space travel, television and VCR — I could go on and on. But not plumbing. That, we are still doing the same way some d___ Roman thought up 2,000 years ago...and he must have been a retarded Roman to boot. There is definitely room here for someone to make their fortune by inventing new and improved methods.

Anyway, Plum just wouldn't leave it alone. Partly, I suspect, because some of the neighbors have already put their toilets in.

"We have a lovely outhouse," I told her; "So indoor toilet is not even on my list in the near future." But she fooled me. One day, she sat down beside me on our sun deck — where I was soaking up some rays, while tapping at the lap top computer's keyboard...from time to time.

She looked dirty, sweaty and disheveled. In a firm tone of voice, she announced, "Well, I have the drain field dug and a trench excavated from under the middle of the house out to the drain field. Now it's time to get some pipe and a toilet."

From the set look on her face, I knew there was no getting out of it — I was stuck. With a sigh, I resigned myself.

Next trip to town, we bought the pipe, fittings and toilet. But, you know what? Not only is the methodology barbaric, but some of the terminology doesn't even make sense...I needed a pipe nipple, they said, handing me a plain piece of pipe threaded on both ends. It certainly didn't look like a nipple to me . But what do I know about plumbing?

The clerks at the store were very helpful, though...and I was relieved that we got away for less than a thousand.

I'll spare you the painful details of installation. It is sufficient to say that we got it all installed, except, at the last, for a foot valve on the intake pipe in the well. I forgot the foot valve. Now I had to take the pipe back off the pump and back out of the well.

The grey plastic intake pipe hung up in the well, on a coupling joint, I suppose. Already angry and frustrated, I grabbed ahold of it with both hands, braced myself, and yanked again — mightily. The pipe flew into the air, with my hands wrapped around it, and past a pipe end projecting from the pump, above, which took generous chunks of flesh from several knuckles. Of course, Plum complained about the blood stains, as she patched me up...I didn't quite bleed to death, though I feared I might.

Having spent so much time on the river over the years, I've been forced to soak up a little knowledge of plumbing, carpentry and mechanics.

I remember the time, another boater had sunk. Plum and I stopped and helped him drag the boat far enough above the surface of the river for the water to be pumped out. He stood in the water to drain the engine, then began to test for spark by holding the spark plugs against the engine, while I turned over the key.

Suddenly, he threw his hands in the air — just like a fervent worshiper at a revival meeting. His hair stood on end, and he whooped, "Yeee-haw! We got fire."

From this experience, I took a lesson about standing in water while working with electricity.

Anyway, Plum has her indoor toilet. It works pretty good, too.

MAYONNAISE AND OTHER FANCY WORDS

It sure is mighty hard to keep up with all this modern scientific eco-terminology. What is this ozone stuff, for instance?

Back in August, I was doing a little cabinet work, building new cabinets for Plum's kitchen, when I heard giggling and carrying on up on the roof. I put aside my finishing chain-saw and went to investigate.

Our daughter, little Plum, was visiting and I could hear her talking to Plum as I backed across the yard to a point where I could see up there. Yup, there they were, both on the roof.

To my amazement, I saw Plum reach into a case full of cans of hair spray and bring out another can. She and Little Plum were saturating the roof with hair spray, carefully covering every square inch of it.

"What in the world are you doing?" I bellowed, calmly, of course.

"Well," Plum said, "You just put this new roof on, and at the lumber store they told me that it was ozone that caused the old roof to rot...So..."

I understood, believe it or not. The light dawned. I am even beginning to understand Plum's thinking. Isn't that scary?

She confirmed it. She had been reading about how hair spray destroys ozone, so logically it should protect the roof. And little Plum backed her up. She said it sounded ok to her that hair spray would protect the roof from ozone.

How could I argue? Evidently, the ozone in the atmosphere hasn't been destroyed at all. It just all fell out of the sky and attacked the tar-paper and rubber roofs.

I was so rattled that, when I went back to my cabinet work, I nearly grabbed up my rough cut chain saw instead of the little finishing one.

And what about this global warming that everybody has been carrying on about for the last couple years? I recall the first time I heard it mentioned. It was back during the winter of eighty-nine. On the radio, the man was talking about our global warming problem. It is going to be a catastrophic disaster, he proclaimed, in tones of doom.

Catastrophic? I am a simple man, not much given to fancy words. Mayonnaise is a real mouthful... to say and understand I mean. But from his tone I gathered that it meant something bad.

I glanced out the window at my thermometer, a fine precision instrument. Mickey's hand pointed unwaveringly at minus sixty-six. Yup, the thought of global warming terrified me.

The weather pattern this last year hasn't done much to change my opinion of global warming. I wonder if a warm up of five degrees or so would really be all that bad. Today, for instance, it would be minus forty instead of minus forty-five. And this fall the snow might not have come until September fifteenth, instead of on the tenth. That does sound like a major problem.

I just don't know. It is all just too much of a strain on my brain. I think I will just gather up my shotgun, and go after those grouse I saw out back. A mess of grouse would go good for dinner, and the fresh air might clear my mind.

PLUM SPEAKS

Our banker, Gary Roth of Denali State Bank, who helped make this book possible, thought it should be titled "ME AND PLUM" since Ted's fabrications (my word, not Gary's) about me occur throughout. Fabrications? Well...all right, maybe there is a kernel of truth at the heart of each story...but how the lazy thing does exagerate.

I see that Ted has mentioned some of our many friends on the Salcha River in these stories. I can only hope that they are still friends after reading this book. I can't mention everyone here but would like to especially mention Betty Redfern and Ida Sanford who have been my closest friends over the last 30 years, or so, and thank them for their supportiveness. And to all our other friends on the Salcha and in North Pole and Fairbanks...many thanks for all your help and all the good times over the years.

And to our kids, Mark and Amy, who Dad verbally abuses in some of these stories (but only in fun). I love you and I'll always be your Dottie.

I would like to give a special acknowledgement and thanks to the three editors/publishers that gave Ted his first breaks in writing: George Piaskowski (THE CURRENT DRIFT)
Rick Coursey (The NORTH POLE INDEPENDENT)
Evan Swensen (ALASKA OUTDOORS)

Thanks to my brother-in-law Russell Pritchett, the attorney, and our excellent editor, Ann Chandonnet, for all their help. And, finally, Thanks to my sister Ruth Cope for taking such good care of our mother, so that I can continue living in Alaska, to help support Ted in the style that he would like to become accustomed to; and so he can continue to act like he's busy writing.

Sincerely, Plum

DEATH IN THE AFTERNOON

She is tense, nervous. This baby will be the first, for the young Alaskan mother ...and she senses that is it is coming soon...right here beside this trail across the tundra.

Preoccupied with the onset of labor, she does not sense the evil presence until too late. The wolves are on her, with a sudden rush.

The old, grey pack leader rips her legs, severing the ham strings, with two swift, slashing bites. A proven maneuver, this, perfected by long practice of generations of wolves.

A scream of pain and terror shatters the silent arctic air, as the young mother collapses. Her legs are useless.

Snarling, the pack rip open her belly, tear out her guts, and pull her baby from her womb, in a gush of crimson blood. Rending fangs tear her baby to bits of tender meat, quickly devoured. They then begin to eat her stomach.

Mercifully, consciousness finally fades into blackness, then death. The patch of spring snow, now crimson, steams awhile, slowly cooling. Red rays of the setting sun creep across the snow to mingle with the red stains of blood.

On the average, 87.5% of all sheep, moose and caribou die this way...eaten alive by wolves or bears. Another 10% die of accidents and disease. A mere

2.5% are harvested for food by human hunters, a quick and merciful death. Prey animals don't die in their bed of old age.

Wolves and bears kill the animals most easily killed...pregnant cows or young calves. They kill more than fifty percent of moose and caribou calves before age six months and, in recent years, fewer than twenty percent of calves live to be one year old, because of predators.

The populations of moose, sheep and caribou are in serious trouble, largely because people ignorant of wildlife biology have interfered with rational management of wolves and bears.

I'm ending this collection with a tragedy and a political note because I love the Alaskan lifestyle and I love the friendly moose, caribou and sheep who share my forest. It's a pleasure to see them around. Now they are endangered...and so is my lifestyle and livelihood, all to suit the whims of a fanatic few radical environmentalists / animal rightists.

Plum and I hope our stories have given you a sense of the warmth and humor of normal, average Alaskans and of why we value our life style that will help you disregard anti-Alaskan propoganda. We do not ask to tell folks in other places how to live and ask a similar respect for our right to live our own way.

AFTERWORD

In our "neighborhood" of the Salcha, along about a five mile stretch of river, we have helped each other build our cabins, pound down wells (we do it by hand), retrieve or repair broken equipment and do many other projects. As a result, we have ended up with a close feeling of family amongst us. Besides ourselves, the members of the "family" are Dewey and Alma Widdis, Rose and Roger Anderson, Sid and Ida Sanford (Sid is one of this book's cover men, sort of like Fabio), Louise McManus, Rick and Dodie Sanders, Roger and Betty Redfern, Dick and Helen Simpkin (the first time I met them, they were helping me pull my sunken boat out of the river), Buck and Ardena Morway and John and Roxanne Braham (John is our local volunteer med-evac pilot).

Further down stream...in the story of my first boat trip on the Salcha I mentioned my rescue by Butch Hayes, who is known for his gruff exterior, an image he fosters. The second time I met Butch and Mary, I asked, "How are you?"

Butch barked, "Meaner than hell!"...seemed serious, too. Underneath the gruff exterior, though he is embarrased to have anyone discover his secret, lurks a heart of gold.

Whenever anyone along the river ran into trouble,

they could count on Butch to lend a helping hand. One time, Butch helped out two boatloads of people who had been in a wreck...a head on collision. One of the participants in the wreck later reported, "Things were in a real mess but after the policeman (Butch) got there it was ok."

We were to discover that eager helpfulness is characteristic of Alaskans in the bush. That helpfulness sometimes makes a life or death difference.

Night Runner, as John Vogt is called on the C.B. radio, got his name from his many journeys through the dark to rescue boaters who had come to grief in the gathering dusk. And most people on the Salcha River have, at one time or another, gratefully looked on professional mechanic Roger Redfern's cheery smile and heard his, "What's your troubles, bubbles?" Roger's C.B. handle is "Shade Tree" because so much of his work seems to be done along the bank of a river under a shade tree.

There are too many others to mention here but the Salcha River "gang" is a good bunch of people.

ALASKAN
WILD LIFE

HUMOROUS PERSPECTIVES
ON LIFE IN THE BUSH

WRITTEN BY TED LEONARD
ILLUSTRATED BY CHAD CARPENTER

Ted Leonard, seen here fleeing a mixed mob of critics, creditors and I.R.S. agents, is the author of another collection of Alaskan humor, ALASKAN WILD LIFE, two Alaskan novels (see page 159), an illustrated collection of Alaskan poetry ARE WE HAVING FUN YET? as well as numerous columns for several Alaskan newspapers. ALASKAN WILD LIFE, ISBN 0-9641553-3-8 can be ordered from Ted Leonard at the address below for $12.00 which includes all postage and handling. Additional copies of NOW WE'RE HAVING FUN can also be ordered for $12.00 including postage and handling.   (prices may change in the future, depending on production costs)

ARE WE HAVING
FUN YET!?!

- For better or verse -
Ted's collected Alaskan poetry

Written by Ted Leonard

A 64 page collection of Alaskan poetry includes 16 great illustrations done by Chad Carpenter, creator of TUNDRA, and Jamie Smith, creator of FREEZE FRAMES
ARE WE HAVING FUN YET?
ISBN 0-9641553-4-6, 64 pages — ask for it at your local book store. Or order direct from Ted Leonard at PO Box 51, Salcha, Alaska 99714. Send only $8.00 (includes postage and handling.) No CODs please. Yes, Ted accepts plastic - include your account number and whether MasterCard or VISA

Ted Leonard has written two books of Alaskan humor, NOW! WE'RE HAVING FUN and ALASKAN WILD LIFE, and an illustrated Alaskan poetry collection ARE WE HAVING FUN YET? See page 158 for more information on these books and ordering information on all Ted's books. Ted has also written two Alaskan novels:

Neath the Midnight Sun $10.00 including postage & handling

A restless breed settled America, traveling across the country ahead of civilization. There has always been a frontier for free spirited individuals who can't tolerate the regimentation, restrictions and crowding of urban civilization.

NEATH THE MIDNIGHT SUN is a story of Alaska, America's last frontier... an adventure... and a romance... and, most of all, a look at how some free spirited Alaskans live, how they think.

Bush pilots and trappers, commercial fishermen and wilderness poets, smugglers, artists and tour guides... The action ranges from the vast wild expanses of Interior Alaska to the blue waters of Kachemak Bay, cupped among rugged, glacier laden mountains, topped by flame shot plumes of volcanic ash.

And, it's the story of Kirk... Kirk. Decorated war hero. Popular bush pilot. Smuggler. And, finally, murderer. The women who loved him. The women he betrayed.

Alaskan Mail-order Bride $12.00 including postage & handling

Mail order brides — ads for them are everywhere, in "scandal magazines", in your home town newspapers across the United States, in trade journals, in the rural electric co-op's monthly magazine... And there's even a magazine, ALASKA MEN, that features eligible Alaskan bachelors.

Do women ever respond to these ads? What are the resulting relationships like?

A NOVEL ABOUT CULTURE SHOCK

As they traveled the narrow wilderness path cross country to their home, Annie's handsome new husband, Kent suddenly seemed slightly sinister, a gun toting stranger.

Across several creeks, deep in the forest, the path ended at his rustic cabin. Wet and cold from a tumble into the creek, frightened by confrontation with a moose along the trail, Annie shivered and stared in dismay at the primitive cabin that loomed, dark and forbidding, from the night. She felt vulnerable and alone — trapped in the sub-Arctic wilderness, amongst wolves and bears, and at the mercy of a stranger. Could she be happy here? Did she have what it takes to be a good wife in this forbidding land? (future prices of these books may change without notice)

SugarPlum, the wife, in front of the Leonard cabin 55 river miles up the Salcha River from the nearest road, the Richardson highway, which crosses the Salcha River 45 miles south of Fairbanks.

At right, Ted shows off his trapper's hat made of marten fur and his leather parka with wolf ruff.

Avid hunters and fishermen, Ted and Plum spend most of their time at their Salcha River cabin.

In addition to his novels, ALASKAN MAIL-ORDER BRIDES and NEATH THE MIDNIGHT SUN and humor books, Ted is a newspaper columnist and an award winning poet.

Ted's photograph is by Nelson's Professional Photography, 606 Bentley Drive, Fairbanks, Alaska.